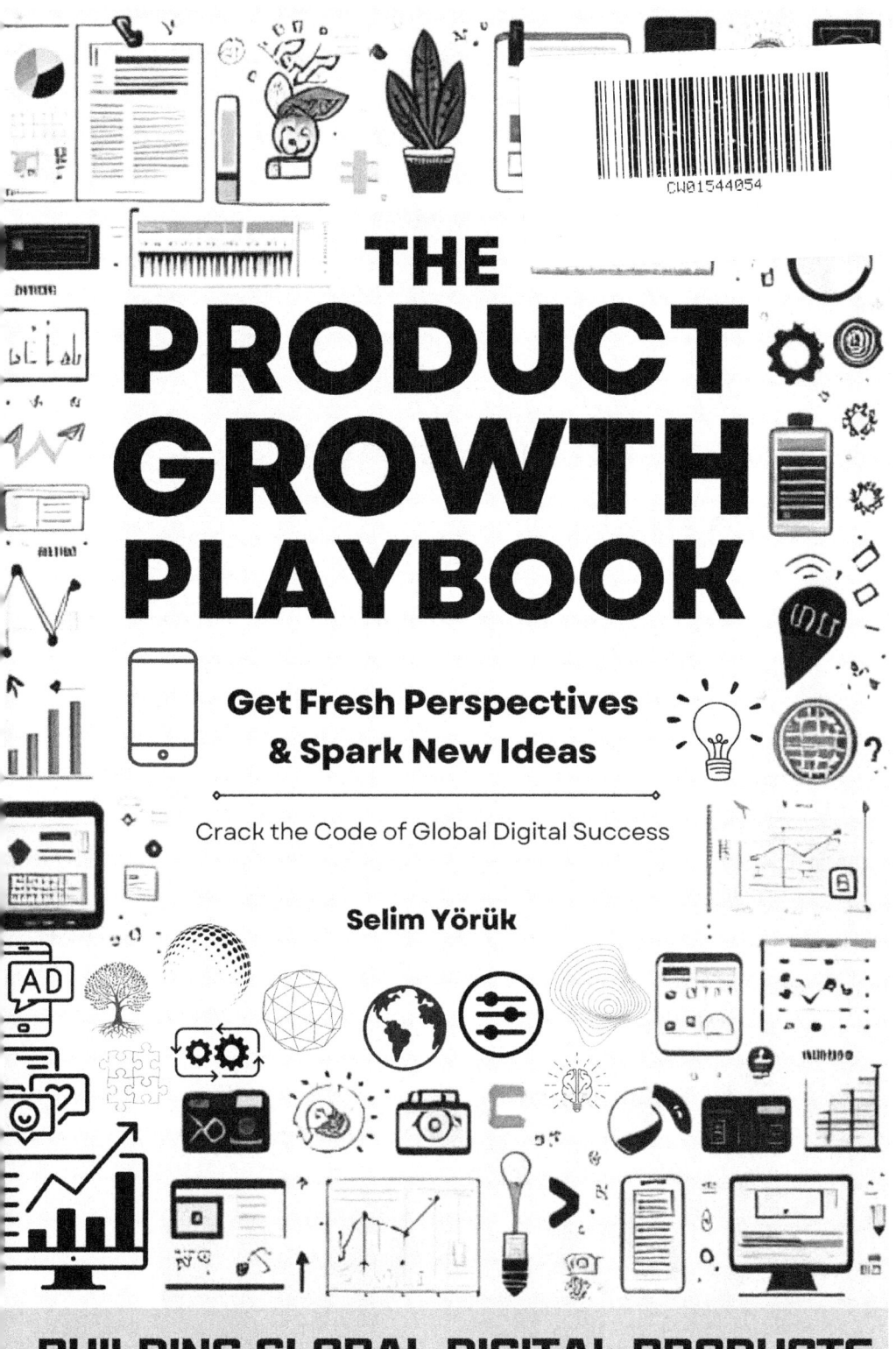

The Product Growth Playbook

Building Global Digital Products: *Get Fresh Perspectives & Spark New Ideas*

By Selim Yoruk

About Author

Selim Yörük, born in Aydın, Türkiye in 1982, engaged in various software projects during his education at Bosphorus University and later co-founded the start-up 4play with a focus on mobile technology and subscription services. This venture quickly gained traction, establishing **Turkcell** as a key business partner. Notably, 4play's Tonla Kazan service earned the prestigious "*Best Mobile Advertising Service*" award from **GSMA**, recognized as the Oscars of the mobile world. The start-up received over 10 global awards for its diverse array of services and apps.

Founded with the vision of B2C Global mobile application development, Madduck, led by Yörük, has seen significant success. The products developed by Madduck's dedicated team have consistently ranked among the top 10 apps in the **Apple** App Store in over 20 countries, including the United States, England, Japan, Israel, and South Korea.

Currently, Selim Yörük plays a pivotal role in the revenue management and marketing of Madduck's innovative products, contributing to the company's global recognition.

Contact: E-mail, Linkedin, X@anafikir

Dedicated to my grandmother, Şekibe, who introduced me to the essence of life.

To my beloved daughter, Nil, who <u>reintroduced</u> me to the essence of life.

And to my home (my wife), Gül...

Foreword: From Notes to a Playbook 9

How to Use This Book: A Companion for Your Product Journey 11

Before You Start Your Startup Adventure 14

- 1 – If You Are a Student or a Recent Graduate; Do Not Start! 15
- 2 – Do Not Quit Your Job 18
- 3 – Not a Start-up, You are a Small Business 20
- 4 – Family First: Building Emotional Capital Before Financial 23
- 5 – Activate Your Resilient Spirit 25
- 6 – First, Start Your Inner Quest 30
- 7 – Define Your True Entrepreneurial Goal 33

How to Find a Creative and Successful Business Idea 36

- 1 – The Persuasion Code: Cracking the Human Mind for Success 37
- 2 – The Problem-Centric Entrepreneur 46
- 3 – Delving Deep into Customer Experiences 52
- 4 – How to Gain In-Depth Market Insights 58
- 5 – Master the Art of Competitive Intelligence 63
- 6 – Building on Proven Concepts 69
- 7 – The Acquisition Advantage 77
- 8 – How to Generate Business Ideas that Sell 84
- 9 – Taming the Idea Jungle: Best Idea to Pursue? 89

Design Revenue-Generating Business Model 94

- 1 – Differentiate to Dominate 96
- 2 – Craft Your Business Model 105
- 3 – Hidden Revenue Streams 117
- 4 – The Cost-Cutting Ninja 122
- 5 – How to Set Key Performance Indicators 127
- 6 – Build Profitable Pricing Models 133
- 7 – Words that Sell: The Power of Persuasive Copywriting 140
- 8 – Validate Your Product Idea Before You Build It 150
- 9 – Pivot from Stagnation to Success 157

Developing a Product That Users Will Fall in Love With 163

- 1 – Build & Manage a Winning Team 164

- 2 – How to Build a Minimum Viable Product 176
- 3 – Crafting User Flows that Flow 182
- 4 – Wireframing: More than Just Sketches 188
- 5 – How to Create Impactful UX & UI 191
- 6 – Birthing a Brand: Perfect-Fit Product Naming 195
- 7 – MVP: The Antidote to Perfection Paralysis 199
- 8 – Unlock Customer Satisfaction with User Testing 202
- 9 – How to Master Post-Launch Management 207

Powerful Marketing Tactics for Explosive Growth **211**
- 1 – Treating Customers Individually Through Segmentation 212
- 2 – Test Your Marketing Channels 215
- 3 – The Missing Ingredient in Your Marketing Strategy 220
- 4 – Cultivating Loyal Fans for Your Brand 226
- 5 – Unlocking the Power of Organic Growth 230
- 6 – Leveraging Partnerships for Business Growth 234
- 7 – Unleashing Revenue Potential 237
- 8 – Optimize to Thrive: Change, Correct, Renew, Update 241

Mastering the Challenges of Global Success **246**
- 1 – Globalize Your Growth 247
- 2 – How to Choose the Right Country for International Expansion 252
- 3 – Subscription Power: Growth & Recurring Profits 255
- 4 – Make a Mobile App 264
- 5 – Make a Mobile Game 279
- 6 – Securing Investment for Your Product 291
- 7 – Mastering Your Money in the Global Market 298

Tools & Resources for Aspiring Entrepreneurs **302**
- 1 – Idea Development Tools 303
- 2 – User Experience and Design Tools 305
- 3 – Software Development Tools 307
- 4 – Project Management Tools 309
- 5 – Marketing Tools 312

Global Entrepreneur's Library **315**

Foreword: From Notes to a Playbook

Welcome adventurers, visionaries, and creators! This is not merely a book; it's the Product Growth Playbook: a gateway to crafting winning digital products and a potent catalyst for sparking new ideas and fostering fresh perspectives.

Within these pages lies a treasure trove of insights, extracted from the fertile grounds of real-world experience, not sterile boardroom theory. It's a culmination of invaluable knowledge honed in the exhilarating trenches of digital product development, where innovation dances with determination.

Believe it or not, this Playbook began as informal notes - scribbles exchanged among colleagues, charting a collective course through the ever-shifting landscape of technology. Yet, these simple notes revealed their profound potential, resonating with colleagues who saw their versatility and far-reaching applicability.

Thus, the whispers of shared knowledge matured into a comprehensive guide, a chronicle of victories and lessons learned, of proven strategies and insightful narratives. It's a testament to the collaborative spirit that fuels progress, an ongoing conversation where you, the reader, become an active participant.

As you embark on this journey, imagine yourself immersed in the heart of a dynamic environment where ideas clash and coalesce, where strategies evolve through tireless iterations, and where groundbreaking products eventually surge to life. Consider this Playbook your trusted guide and companion, a seasoned advisor who offers wisdom drawn not from sterile textbooks, but from the pulsating lifeblood of real-world challenges and triumphs.

May this Playbook empower you to forge your unique path to success, fueled by the insights gleaned from others who have navigated this terrain. It's a catalyst for igniting your imagination, for reshaping perspectives, and ultimately, for propelling you towards the summit of digital product excellence.

Let the journey begin! Embrace the power to create, to innovate, to shape experiences that resonate. Craft those winning products, those digital masterpieces that leave a lasting impact on the world.

The path to creative brilliance often begins with a simple note. Now, turn the page and begin your own epic story of ingenuity and digital victory.

> *"Working hard for something we don't care about is called stress; working hard for something we love is called passion."*
>
> *— Simon Sinek*

How to Use This Book: A Companion for Your Product Journey

Congratulations on embarking on the remarkable journey of creating an international digital product.

Your endeavor is not merely a personal pursuit; it's a beacon of innovation that promises to make a significant impact, not just on your country but also on the global stage.

As you navigate this transformative adventure, remember that you are not alone. This book stands as your unwavering companion, a treasure trove of insights and guidance designed to empower you every step of the way.

While the path ahead may seem daunting, filled with unexpected twists and turns, rest assured that you have the resilience and determination to overcome any obstacle. This book is not a traditional read-from-cover-to-cover tome. Instead, it's a dynamic resource, a problem-solving companion that you can revisit time and again, whenever you encounter a challenge or seek fresh perspectives.

Imagine this book as your trusted advisor, always within reach on your desk, ready to offer its wisdom and guidance. When confronted with a specific hurdle, simply open the relevant section and immerse yourself in the practical suggestions and straightforward guidance.

I understand that your time is precious, and the world of work demands your utmost attention. That's why I've meticulously crafted this book to be as concise and accessible as possible, avoiding unnecessary jargon and complexities. Focus on grasping the core concepts and applying them to your unique situation.

Don't think of this book as a rigid collection of absolute truths; instead, view it as a compilation of "lecture notes" from a close friend who has traversed this path countless times. Let these notes serve as a catalyst for your own thinking, provoking questions and prompting you to delve deeper into the subject matter.

"A prudent question is one-half of wisdom."
— Francis Bacon

The insights contained within these pages are not mere theoretical constructs; they are forged from years of real-world experience, lessons learned from both successes and setbacks. I myself regularly revisit these notes whenever I encounter challenges, and their effectiveness never ceases to amaze me.

Embrace this book as your unwavering companion, a source of inspiration and guidance that will illuminate your path towards creating globally cherished, indispensable, and lucrative products.

Onward, intrepid explorer! May your journey be filled with innovation, resilience, and resounding success.

PLEASE, LEAVE A REVIEW

Honest reviews help readers find the right book for their needs.

To leave a review, please search the name of the book on amazon.com.

Thanks for being part of the journey!

Before You Start Your Startup Adventure

Before starting a global business, take a moment to honestly assess yourself. This journey is not easy and requires making tough decisions.

Make sure you are ready for the challenges ahead, both personally and professionally.

Recognize your strengths and weaknesses, and understand your fears and goals. Are you prepared for the demanding path ahead? Can you handle uncertainty and make changes when needed?

This chapter is a mirror, reflecting the realities of starting a business. It's a reminder to check your commitment and resilience before entering the global market.

▸ 1 – If You Are a Student or a Recent Graduate; Do Not Start!

Congratulations on your graduation! This milestone marks the end of your academic journey and the exciting beginning of a new chapter.

If you're feeling the entrepreneurial spirit stirring within, eager to launch into the startup world with grand ideas, take a moment to consider some crucial aspects.

You're likely brimming with energy, passion, and a belief in your peak creativity. Perhaps you've even experimented with small projects and are dreaming of creating the next tech titan like Facebook or Google.

The thought of escaping the confines of being a typical corporate employee and embracing the idea that real learning comes from making mistakes can be highly motivating.

However, it's important to confront some sobering truths:

- **High Failure Rates of Startups**: The stark reality is that about 90% of startups fail within their first five years. A significant reason for this is a lack of experience in handling unforeseen challenges that arise in the business world.
- **The Reality of Entrepreneurship**: Owning a business isn't always the glamorous, success-laden journey it's

often portrayed as. It's a path filled with demands and challenges that can be more consuming than you might expect.

- **Financial Challenges**: Starting a business isn't just about potential earnings. Especially in the initial years, it often means facing financial losses. It's crucial to consider the opportunity costs and financial implications before diving in.
- **The Power of Networking**: Many successful entrepreneurs attribute a part of their success to strong networking. As a recent graduate, you may not have had the chance to build such a network yet.
- **Bridging the Skill and Knowledge Gap**: Venturing into the business world without a solid understanding of the fundamentals is akin to swimming with sharks without knowing how to swim. It's a risky move that requires careful thought.

Now, before you feel discouraged, here's a more pragmatic approach:

Instead of rushing into starting your own venture, why not first delve into the startup ecosystem?

1. Identify startups in your region that inspire you, particularly those with a global influence or significant international customer base.
2. Reach out to these startup founders, express your admiration, and seek opportunities to work with and learn from them.
3. Aim to spend around six months in each startup, gaining diverse experiences across different markets and business models.

4. After gaining two years of hands-on experience in various startups, reassess your entrepreneurial ambitions. If there are aspects of business you still don't fully grasp, continue this learning process.

In summary; Spend 5-10 years working in various companies that suit your interests in which you plan to establish a company in the future. This period is crucial for learning, gaining experience, and building a strong foundation for your future venture.

Patience and persistent learning are key to preparing yourself for the challenging yet rewarding journey of entrepreneurship.

> *"In business, everyone gets paid two different things: cash and experience. Get experience first; cash comes later."*
>
> *— Harold Geneen*

2 – Do Not Quit Your Job

The allure of entrepreneurship is often painted as the modern-day gold rush, a chance to strike it rich with the mere tools of determination and innovation.

Countless success stories and smiling photos of entrepreneurs at the signing table may have you contemplating quitting your job right away to embark on this thrilling adventure. However, life, much like the gold rush, isn't that simple.

Consider this: not everyone has to be an entrepreneur, and for the majority of society, those who lack a high-risk appetite, entrepreneurship might not be the right path. The notion that being a salaried employee is akin to modern slavery is an oversimplification.

In reality, it's almost impossible to become an expert in something without accumulating years of experience within a company.

Being a startup or company owner doesn't automatically equate to happiness; it often involves blood, sweat, and tears. Beyond the monetary gains, you may have other, more profound dreams about life, and that's perfectly valid.

As emphasized throughout this book, entrepreneurship is a journey of trial and error, akin to scientific experimentation. The process involves forming a theory, conducting tests, adapting to results, and repeating the cycle. Uncertainty is a constant, and success is far from guaranteed.

Entrepreneurship is comparable to stepping onto a suspension bridge for the first time. You step cautiously, testing the solidity of each board beneath your feet, unsure of what lies ahead. It's a proven method with the highest probability of success.

While many advocate for quitting your job to fully dedicate yourself to entrepreneurship, there's a crucial point often overlooked. This advice doesn't necessarily apply to the initial stages of realizing your venture, as outlined in this book. You can test your ideas and business model while maintaining a parallel job.

This dual approach allows you to experiment without risking everything. If the results aren't as anticipated, you can iterate, refine, and try again. Be patient; success often emerges only once out of every ten attempts. Recognizing this, persist in trying until you find the winning formula.

Only when you're confident that your venture has passed all tests successfully, and a genuine opportunity lies ahead, should quitting your job become a consideration. Until then, stay committed to your current work, enhance your expertise, and, if you have a passion for enterprise, keep testing the waters.

Remember, entrepreneurship is not a sprint but a marathon, and the journey is as crucial as the destination.

3 – Not a Start-up, You are a Small Business

In the 17th century, European sailors were captivated by the riches of Southeast Asia, particularly the sought-after sauce known as "kê-tsiap."

As invaders pondered the sauce's allure, they found a way to replicate it, eventually giving birth to the now ubiquitous ketchup.

This historical tale mirrors our modern inclination to be drawn to what's produced in other cultures and distant lands, including business concepts like the American "Start-up."

In many countries, businesses proudly adopt the term *"start-up"* but often, this is nothing more than a superficial desire, akin to using fancy jargon without understanding its essence.

To those who use the term without understanding *"what a start-up truly is"*, let's clarify.

Contrary to popular belief, a start-up is not merely a *"newly established young and dynamic technology-oriented company"*. Instead, it is an **investment tool** born out of a specific need.

The concept emerged because *making money from money* doesn't rely on traditional interest-based methods in many countries. For individuals seeking alternative investment instruments with the potential for substantial returns, the start-up and valuation concepts were born.

However, the context in many countries is different. Economic landscapes are not characterized by the same need for risky, high-return investment instruments. Wealthy individuals often earn through low-risk avenues like interest, real estate, and other stable investments, making the concept of start-ups less applicable.

While there are investors embracing the start-up culture in developing countries, their existence is somewhat miraculous. These individuals, driven by a love for adventure, should be cherished and not offended. However, it's essential to question how many of them have experienced a successful "exit" with a tenfold valuation.

In regions with a thriving start-up culture, businesses are specifically established for the purpose of achieving a tenfold profit. Everything, from business cultures to management practices, is geared towards this goal. The culture of innovation, productivity, and creativity thrives in this environment, fostering the success stories we witness today.

In many countries, businesses often run like traditional enterprises, yet adorn their business cards with the title of "start-up founder". Cultural codes are rooted in vanity, reflected in tendencies to showcase the latest tech gadgets even when making ends meet is a struggle.

Realistically, most businesses fall within a certain profitability range, a far cry from the ambitious goal of multiplying valuation by ten in ten years.

So, perhaps it's time to embrace the identity of a **small business**, acknowledging proximity to a more realistic road ahead.

As a final note, much like the original "kê-tsiap" sauce having nothing to do with tomatoes, true understanding is essential before adopting labels. Pretending to be a start-up without grasping the content is futile.

> *"The business world is full of people who are more interested in appearing important than in doing important things."*
>
> *— Warren Buffett*

4 – Family First: Building Emotional Capital Before Financial

As children, many of us dreamt of becoming astronauts, a dream that was often met with enthusiasm and support from our families.

This childhood ambition, filled with imagination and creativity, symbolizes the kind of big dreams we carry into adulthood, such as starting a business. However, just as our families may have gently guided us towards more pragmatic paths away from becoming astronauts, they might express similar concerns about the entrepreneurial journey.

Before venturing into the world of business, it's critical to not only believe in yourself but also to convince your family and relatives of your vision. Starting a business is a consuming endeavor that will impact not just your life but also the lives of those closest to you.

Your family will experience the highs and lows alongside you, and their support can be a crucial factor in your success.

Establishing and growing a company, achieving success, and expanding globally are endeavors as challenging as the childhood dream of becoming an astronaut. Your family, friends, and the world around you might express doubts and discourage you from venturing into entrepreneurship, similar to how they dissuaded the pursuit of a childhood dream.

Convincing your family and loved ones involves sincere and serious conversations about your dreams, the challenges you anticipate, and the potential benefits not just for you but for them as well. This initial step, often overlooked, is your first investment - not in monetary terms, but in gaining their consent and support.

Even if you believe in your ability to sway future investors, securing the backing of your family, friends, and immediate community is paramount. Their investment may not come with a monetary value, but the **emotional support they provide is priceless**.

In the words of Tony Robbins, "*Business success is 80 per cent psychology and 20 per cent mechanics*". This sentiment underscores the importance of securing the psychological support of those closest to you, as their encouragement and understanding will play a significant role in your entrepreneurial journey.

In conclusion, just as a child's dream of becoming an astronaut often starts and evolves with family support, so does the dream of becoming an entrepreneur.

Gaining the confidence and backing of your family and relatives is a crucial first step in your business venture. It ensures that you have a strong emotional foundation to face the challenges and celebrate the successes of your entrepreneurial journey.

5 – Activate Your Resilient Spirit

Embarking on an entrepreneurial journey is a formidable challenge, requiring not just skill and innovation but, most importantly, resilience.

This quality, above all others, has been the defining factor in the success of many celebrated entrepreneurs. Their stories of persistence, overcoming adversity, and maintaining determination in the face of daunting challenges provide powerful lessons on why resilience is crucial for any successful enterprise.

Steve Jobs: Turning Setbacks into Comebacks

The co-founder of Apple Inc., is a prime example of resilience in the entrepreneurial world. Jobs faced numerous setbacks, including being ousted from the very company he helped create.

However, instead of letting this defeat him, he went on to found NeXT and Pixar, making significant strides in both the computer and animation industries.

His return to Apple marked one of the most extraordinary comebacks in business history. Under his leadership, Apple introduced groundbreaking products like the iPod, iPhone, and iPad, revolutionizing multiple industries.

Jobs' resilience in the face of adversity was key to his and Apple's success.

J.K. Rowling: From Rejection to Global Success

His journey to becoming one of the most successful authors in history is a striking example of resilience. Before "Harry Potter" became a global phenomenon, Rowling faced numerous rejections from publishers, at a time when she was a struggling single mother living on welfare.

Her perseverance paid off when a small publisher took a chance on *"Harry Potter and the Philosopher's Stone"*. The series went on to become a cultural landmark and a best-selling book series, demonstrating Rowling's resilience in overcoming personal and professional obstacles to achieve her dreams.

Elon Musk: Defying Odds in Multiple Industries

The CEO of SpaceX and Tesla, Inc., embodies resilience in the face of seemingly insurmountable odds. Musk faced skepticism and setbacks as he attempted to revolutionize industries dominated by long-established players.

At Tesla, he overcame financial struggles and production challenges to make electric cars mainstream.

With SpaceX, he achieved what many thought impossible for a private company, launching and landing reusable rockets, even winning contracts from NASA.

Musk's resilience, his ability to continue despite numerous failures and criticisms, has been central to his companies' successes.

Entrepreneurs often face the brink of failure, with moments where all seems lost. However, it's resilience that allows them to persevere through these hardships.

Here's a candid look at what lies ahead:

1. **Skyrocketing Responsibilities:** Expect your responsibilities to soar. You'll bear the weight of expectations from various stakeholders, confront the consequences of your decisions on others, and grapple with tasks you'd rather avoid.
2. **Solitude in Struggles:** Loneliness will become a familiar companion. Friends, family, and even loved ones may not fully comprehend the challenges you face. Your struggles will be yours to endure.
3. **Long-Term Financial Strain:** Financial discomfort will be your companion for an extended period. Your standard of living will decline, and the comfort you once knew will fade into the background.
4. **Constant Battles:** You'll find yourself in numerous conflicts–with partners, employees, customers, and even within your personal relationships. Navigating these constant battles will require a resilient spirit.
5. **Self-Doubt Creeps In:** Moments of self-doubt will haunt you. There will be tasks beyond your reach, challenges seemingly insurmountable, making you question your capabilities and worth.
6. **Unforeseen Challenges:** Just when you believe you've devised the perfect plan, unforeseen challenges will

blindside you. Flexibility and adaptability will become your survival tools.
7. **Rock Bottom Beckons:** You'll hit rock bottom—feeling like it's the end, with no escape from the overwhelming burden. Resilience will be your lifeline.
8. **Envy Amidst Fatigue:** As fatigue sets in, you'll look around and envy those seemingly enjoying marvelous lives while you're engulfed in the stress and demands of your venture.
9. **Endless Toil:** Work will consume every waking moment. Even in the dead of night, thoughts of work will invade your mind. Finding time for leisure will become a rare luxury.
10. **Struggle to Sell Your Vision:** Despite your belief in a fantastic product, attracting customers will be an uphill battle. The years may pass without the anticipated success.

Resilience is not just about enduring but also about adapting and growing in the face of challenges. It involves maintaining a vision even when others doubt you, persisting through financial and emotional lows, and turning failures into learning experiences.

Now, the pivotal question arises: Is it worth enduring all this? The answer lies in choosing the right goal. Knowing yourself, understanding your true aspirations, and aligning your goals accordingly will be the compass guiding you through the storm.

Success in entrepreneurship is not guaranteed, but if your goal is authentic and resonates with your true desires, the journey will be its own reward.

The decision to endure this arduous journey and emerge victorious ultimately rests in your hands.

*"**Brilliant thinking is rare, but courage is in even shorter supply than genius.**"*

— Peter Thiel

6 – First, Start Your Inner Quest

Before venturing into the unpredictable landscape of entrepreneurship, there's a crucial journey you must embark on–the journey of self-discovery.

This self-awareness acts as your compass, directing you towards goals that are truly meaningful and fulfilling.

In our lives, it's common to follow in the footsteps of others - be it our parents, friends, or celebrated figures. We often adopt their tastes, preferences, and even their dreams, hoping it will bring us happiness. But it's important to pause and consider two critical questions:

1. **Are the People We Follow Truly Happy?** It can be difficult to truly know if the people we emulate are happy. If they aren't, following their path might not lead us to fulfillment. And even if they are content, it brings us to another important question.
2. **Are Our Soul, Personality, and Truths Aligned with Theirs?** To answer this, we delve into the inner worlds of both ourselves and those we admire. Knowing their stories, biographies, and struggles is the easy part. Unraveling our own soul, personality, and truths is the true challenge.

Do you truly know yourself? Have you explored your inner world–your fears, joys, passions, and idiosyncrasies? Without this self-awareness, defining happiness or success becomes an elusive task, and you risk adopting others' definitions that may lead you astray.

Here's a roadmap for self-discovery:

1. **Ask Yourself More Questions:**
   - What do you enjoy doing?
   - What are your dreams?
   - What legacy do you want to leave?
   - What self-criticisms recur the most?
   - How do you wish others to describe you?
2. **Keep a Diary:** Maintain a diary to capture your recurring thoughts and emotions. Reflecting on these entries provides insights into your inner workings.
3. **Define Your Roles:** Identify the various roles you play in life–parent, friend, leader, mentor, creator. Determine which role brings you the most joy and fulfillment.
4. **List Your Interests:** Enumerate your interests and curiosities. What subjects captivate your attention and consume your time?
5. **Money is No Object:** Imagine having unlimited resources. What would you do every day? This fantasy unveils your true passions.
6. **Explore Personality Tests:** Engage in established personality tests like the 16 Archetypes Test. Understanding your personality type can unravel hidden emotions, motivations, strengths, and weaknesses, guiding you toward fulfilling endeavors.

Self-discovery is a lifelong journey, and there's no one-size-fits-all approach. Embrace the uniqueness of your path. As you unravel the layers of your identity, you'll uncover the authentic desires that will shape a meaningful goal–a goal that transcends external influences and defines your happiness.

> *"Your vision will become clear only when you can look into your own heart. Who looks outside, dreams; who looks inside, awakens."*
>
> *– Carl Gustav Jung*

7 – Define Your True Entrepreneurial Goal

In the world of entrepreneurship, the true value of the journey lies in having a clear and meaningful goal, one that goes beyond just the pursuit of wealth.

Before you dive into the adventure of starting a business, it's important to ask yourself: What significant goal do you aim to achieve in your life?

Think about it like this: Imagine a friend who finds immense joy in driving. For this friend, a car isn't just a way to get from point A to point B; it represents much more–it's a passion, a symbol of freedom, a part of who they are. While most people drive to reach a specific destination, for this friend, the act of driving is the destination itself.

I remember a day when this friend took me on a drive with no clear destination. We drove for hours, and I became increasingly anxious as we traversed unfamiliar roads. I couldn't help but ask a flurry of questions: Where are we going? Why am I here? What will happen when we get there?

During our journey, I came to understand his deep connection with cars. As a child, during times of family conflict or personal struggle, he would seek solace in his car. It was more than just a vehicle; it was a refuge, a place where he could escape challenges, find peace, and feel safe from judgment.

Similarly, your dream of starting a business, being your own boss, or creating something unique might be akin to this friend's passion for driving. It might represent a way to break free from early mornings, financial struggles, answering to a boss, or feelings of inadequacy.

But here's the key question: Is your dream of entrepreneurship truly aligned with a meaningful goal, or is it simply a means to escape life's difficulties? This distinction is crucial in determining the authenticity and potential success of your entrepreneurial endeavor.

When to Start a Company:

You should contemplate starting a company when your life's goal aligns with the pursuit of entrepreneurship and when it becomes the most direct path to realizing that goal.

Consider these examples of beautiful life goals that might warrant starting a company:

1. **Empowering Others:** Enabling at least 1 million people to accomplish tasks more efficiently, affordably, or quickly.
2. **Work-Life Balance:** Reducing weekly working hours to 20 without compromising one's standard of living, fostering more time with family and personal pursuits.
3. **Passionate Pursuits:** Engaging in work that sparks excitement and happiness, with at least 8 out of every 10 mornings filled with enthusiasm.
4. **People-Centric Success:** Providing excellent salaries to at least 100 individuals whose personalities resonate with your values.

5. **Global Impact:** Achieving acquisition by a global company or contributing 10% of earnings to benefit those in Africa facing preventable challenges.

If starting a company doesn't significantly contribute to achieving your life goals, reconsider burdening yourself and those you work with.

Navigating the Entrepreneurial Journey:

Running a company is akin to driving a car. If you don't know where you're going, the journey becomes a torment for you and those involved. Knowing your destination simplifies decision-making.

Imagine the road changes or an obstacle appears. What will you do? Without a clear destination, decisions become arbitrary, leading you to unintended places. When your destination is clear, every decision becomes straightforward.

In challenging moments, the crucial question to ask is, "*Which option will make it easier or faster for me to reach my goal?*" With a clear goal, you can navigate the twists and turns of entrepreneurship purposefully.

How to Find a Creative and Successful Business Idea

In this segment, we delve into the art of uncovering business ideas with the potential for global success.

It's not just about generating ideas; it's about discerning their proximity to success and determining the optimal starting point if you're juggling multiple concepts.

A successful business idea serves as the cornerstone of any entrepreneurial venture, and here, we equip you with the tools to objectively evaluate your brainchild, ensuring you make pragmatic decisions without becoming enamored with a singular idea.

Understanding that a business idea is the catalyst for all entrepreneurial endeavors, we guide you through a comprehensive exploration. We decipher the factors that distinguish an idea with global appeal, helping you discern its viability.

Moreover, for those blessed with a surplus of ideas, we unravel the conundrum of prioritization, aiding you in choosing which concept merits initiation first.

The key lies not just in having an idea but in scrutinizing it with a discerning eye, paving the way for informed and strategic decisions as you embark on the exciting journey of entrepreneurial innovation.

1 – The Persuasion Code: Cracking the Human Mind for Success

When you have a brilliant idea that sparks your passion and seems to promise great success, it's easy to get caught up in the excitement.

Here's a reality check: often, no one in the world is as excited about your idea as you are. Not investors, not your family, not even your closest friends.

This doesn't mean your idea isn't good, but it does mean you need to take a step back to evaluate and strategize before diving in.

Before you embark on turning your idea into reality, there's a crucial step to take: put your idea to the side.

Up until now, you've been the sole audience for your idea. You've sold it to yourself, reveling in its brilliance. However, the real challenge lies in convincing others.

Convincing others or selling a product/service/idea involves two key approaches:

1. **Create Change:** You can demonstrate how your offering will alter someone's life.
2. **Inspire Hope:** If your idea isn't directly causing change, you can instead sell the promise or potential of change.

Without either of these elements, you're unlikely to sway or persuade anyone.

In the art of communication, persuasion stands as one of the most powerful tools. It's the subtle art and science of influence that shapes opinions, decisions, and actions.

Whether it's a marketer convincing a customer, a leader rallying a team, or a friend swaying another's opinion, the ability to persuade effectively is invaluable in navigating the complexities of our social and professional lives.

The effectiveness of persuasion is deeply rooted in understanding human psychology. To truly master the art of persuasion, it's essential to grasp the psychological principles that influence how people think, feel, and act.

One of the most influential frameworks in this context is the principles of influence developed by **Dr. Robert Cialdini**. Let's explore these principles and how they form the bedrock of persuasive tactics.

1. Reciprocity

The principle of reciprocity is based on the notion that people feel obliged to return favors.

When someone does something for us, we naturally want to repay them in kind. In persuasion, this can be as simple as offering a small gift or favor, which can create a sense of obligation in the recipient to respond positively to your request.

2. Commitment and Consistency

People like to be seen as consistent in their actions and beliefs. Once we commit to something, whether verbally or in writing, we are more likely to follow through with it.

Persuasion strategies leveraging this principle often involve getting an initial, small commitment, which then leads to larger commitments.

3. Social Proof

We are social creatures and often look to others to determine what is correct or desirable. This principle, known as social proof, suggests that people are more likely to do something if they see others doing it.

Testimonials, customer reviews, and endorsements are examples of using social proof in persuasion.

4. Authority

People tend to respect and follow the lead of legitimate authorities. Demonstrating expertise or establishing credibility in a given area can make your persuasive efforts more effective.

This is why experts in a field, or even individuals in positions of power, can influence others more easily.

5. Liking

We are more easily persuaded by people we like. Factors that contribute to liking include physical attractiveness, similarity, compliments, and cooperative endeavors. Persuaders often build rapport and find common ground with their audience to enhance their likability.

6. Scarcity

The principle of scarcity is based on the idea that limited availability increases desirability. People are more likely to want something if they believe it's in short supply.

Marketers often use this principle by creating a sense of urgency or exclusivity around a product or service.

Understanding these principles offers a window into the human mind, revealing why certain persuasive techniques are effective. However, it's important to note that these principles should be applied ethically and responsibly. Misuse can lead to manipulation, eroding trust and credibility.

Effective persuasion involves a careful balance between emotional appeal and logical reasoning. Understanding how to harmonize these elements is key to influencing others.

Emotion: The Heart of Persuasion

- Emotional Connection: Emotions like fear, joy, and hope can strongly motivate people. Emotional storytelling in advertising, for example, creates a connection with the audience.
- Risks of Over-Emotionalizing: Relying too much on emotion without substantial content can lead to skepticism.

Logic: The Rational Side

- Facts and Evidence: Logical persuasion uses data and factual arguments. This is effective in contexts where decisions are based on objective criteria.
- Avoiding Logical Fallacies: Beware of logical fallacies, as they can undermine your argument's credibility.

Balancing the Two

- Know Your Audience: Tailor your approach based on whether your audience prefers emotional narratives or logical arguments.

- **Integrating Both Elements**: The most compelling messages often combine emotional and logical elements. For instance, a health campaign might use statistics (logic) alongside personal stories (emotion).

The integration of emotion and logic can greatly enhance the impact of your persuasive efforts.

Storytelling and the use of metaphors are potent tools in the arsenal of persuasion. They have the unique ability to simplify complex ideas, evoke emotions, and create a memorable impact on the audience.

Storytelling: Humanizing Your Message

- **Relatability**: Stories allow your audience to see themselves in the narrative, making your message more relatable and impactful. For example, a brand story that shares the struggles and triumphs of a company can create a deeper connection with customers.
- **Memorability**: Humans are naturally wired to remember stories. A well-told story can make your message stick in the audience's mind long after the facts and figures have faded.
- **Emotional Engagement**: Stories often engage the audience emotionally, making them feel part of the journey. This emotional investment can significantly influence attitudes and decisions.

Metaphors: Simplifying Complex Concepts

- **Conceptual Understanding**: Metaphors can translate complex or abstract concepts into simpler, more tangible

terms. In business presentations, metaphors can be used to explain intricate processes or strategies in a way that's easier to grasp.
- **Enhancing Persuasiveness**: A well-chosen metaphor can add strength to your argument by drawing parallels that resonate with the audience. It can also make your message more vivid and engaging.

Combining Storytelling and Metaphors

- **Synergy**: When used together, storytelling and metaphors can create a powerful synergy. A metaphor woven into a story can drive the point home more effectively.
- **Context Matters**: The key is to choose stories and metaphors that align with your audience's experiences and the message you want to convey.

Mastering the art of storytelling and the strategic use of metaphors can elevate your persuasive communication.

They not only make your message more engaging and understandable but also ensure that it resonates deeply with your audience.

Consider the scenario where you enthusiastically share your groundbreaking idea with your loved ones. Instead of receiving the anticipated applause, you're met with indifference or skepticism. Your girlfriend looks unimpressed, your father advises you to focus on your job, and even finding an investor becomes an uphill battle.

The truth is, no one is inherently interested in your idea. To make your case, you must tailor your approach to your audience:

- To win over your lover, paint a vivid picture of the incredible life you'll lead together with this business idea.
- To convince your father, speak to the pride he'll feel in your accomplishments with this idea.
- When facing an investor, start with a compelling proposition–highlight the potential for a million-dollar valuation with minimal investment.

Yet, the most critical person to convince is the future customer.

Understanding the Customer:

If your idea hasn't gone beyond the realm of "Wouldn't it be great if this happened," it's time to pause and put your idea down gently. Before you can pitch it effectively, you need to ask and answer essential questions:

- *Who will buy this product or service?*
- *Why would they buy it?*
- *How will it change their lives?*
- *Is it worth the price you're asking?*
- *Does it solve a genuine problem for them?*
- *Do they perceive the problem as significant enough to warrant a solution?*

Without comprehensive answers to these questions, your idea remains in its infancy. This is precisely where the idea section of this guide comes into play.

By understanding your audience–whether it's your lover, your father, an investor, or most importantly, your future customer–you'll be better equipped to navigate the journey from idea to reality.

"The best way to differentiate yourself is to understand your customers better than anyone else."

— Tony Hsieh

2 – The Problem-Centric Entrepreneur

Venturing onto the path of ideation demands a meticulous exploration of your potential customers, their needs, and the segments where your expertise can make a significant impact.

Successful business ideas are rooted in solving authentic problems faced by real customers. To initiate this journey, temporarily set aside preconceived notions and adopt an objective stance, focusing on aligning your offerings with the most pressing needs of your target audience.

Key Steps:

1. **Set Aside Your Initial Idea**: Begin by temporarily putting your current idea aside. This allows for an unbiased approach in the following steps.
2. **Self-Discovery**: Engage in a process of self-discovery. Understand your strengths, passions, and values to ensure your idea aligns with who you are.
3. **Define Your Goal**: Clearly set your goal. What do you want to achieve with your idea? Having a clear objective will guide your ideation process.
4. **Identify Experienced Customer Segments**: Make a list of customer segments you have previously served and have experience with. Understanding your past interactions can offer valuable insights.
5. **Identify Personal Experience Segments**: List the market segments where you are a customer yourself.

Personal experiences as a customer can provide unique perspectives.
6. **Eliminate Unpreferred Segments**: Review your list and cross off any customer segments that you wouldn't enjoy serving. Focus on those you are passionate about.
7. **Prioritize Similar Segments**: Identify which of these customer segments closely align with your skills and interests. Place these at the top of your list, as mentioned in Article 2.
8. **Align Customers with Your Goal**: Think about which remaining customer segments can help you achieve your goal (set in step 3) in the easiest and fastest way. Reorder them accordingly.
9. **List Customer Problems**: Start a new list of problems faced by each customer segment, beginning with the one at the top of your list. This focuses your idea on solving real-world issues.
10. **Create a Problem Notebook**: Instead of trying to list all problems in one sitting, develop a habit of noting down problems as you encounter them in everyday life. Treat this as an ongoing problem notebook, not just a one-time list.

Thought-Provoking Questions:

1. **Spending Habits**: "What do customers spend the most money on? Understanding their spending priorities can highlight significant issues."
2. **Time Allocation**: "What activities or tasks consume most of their time? This can indicate areas of inefficiency or frustration."

3. **Common Complaints**: "What are the biggest complaints or pain points customers have? These are often clear indicators of problems needing solutions."
4. **Industry Analysis**: "Reflect on the industry you have experience in. What persistent problems have existed for the last five years and continue to this day?"
5. **Emotional Challenges**: "Could mood-related issues, such as boredom, depression, or loneliness, be potential problems for customers?"
6. **Problem Significance**: "How important are the problems I've identified? Typically, the more crucial a problem is, the more willing customers are to spend money on a solution."
7. **Frequency of Problems**: "How often do these problems occur? Issues that arise daily or are hard to ignore are more likely to drive customers to seek solutions than those that are infrequent."
8. **Prevalence of the Problem**: "How many people share the same problem? Commercial viability often depends on the problem being widespread."
9. **Financial Capacity of Customers**: "Do the customers experiencing this problem have the financial means to spend on a solution?"
10. **Competitive Landscape**: "Are other companies attempting to solve this problem? If so, why hasn't it been resolved yet? Understanding the gap in current solutions can reveal opportunities."

As entrepreneur Paul Marsden aptly put it, "Business is solving other people's problems–for money."

This strategic, customer-centric approach not only guides your ideation process but positions your business for genuine impact and success.

The path to groundbreaking startup ideas often lies in the profound understanding and resolution of authentic problems.

Inspiring Business Tales:

✳ **Tinder's Swipe-to-Like Dating (2012):**
Tinder identified the complexities of online dating and the time-consuming nature of creating detailed profiles. Simplifying the process, they introduced the swipe-to-like feature, making it easy for users to connect with potential matches based on mutual interest. This user-friendly approach revolutionized the online dating landscape.

✳ **Warby Parker's Online Glasses Shopping (2010):**
Warby Parker founders recognized the inconvenience and high prices associated with buying eyeglasses. They disrupted the eyewear industry by offering affordable, stylish glasses online and allowing customers to try them at home for free. This customer-centric approach challenged the status quo of traditional brick-and-mortar eyewear retailers.

✳ **Nintendo's Wii Gaming Console (2006):**
Nintendo observed that traditional gaming consoles were often intimidating for non-gamers. To address this, they developed the Wii with motion-sensing controllers, making gaming accessible and enjoyable for a broader audience. The

innovative approach transformed the gaming industry and expanded the market.

* **Waze's Crowdsourced Navigation (2008):**
Waze was born out of frustration with traditional navigation apps not providing real-time traffic information. Leveraging crowdsourcing, Waze allows users to share real-time traffic and road information. This customer-centric model has made Waze a go-to navigation app, demonstrating the power of collective user input.

* **Spotify's Personalized Playlists (2008):**
Spotify observed users struggling with creating personalized playlists. In response, they introduced algorithms that analyzed users' listening habits to curate personalized playlists like Discover Weekly. This move not only alleviated the burden of manual playlist creation but also kept users engaged by delivering music tailored to their preferences.

"Your customers don't care about you. They don't care about your product or service. They care about themselves, their dreams, and their goals.

Now, they will care much more if you help them reach their goals, and to do that, you must understand their goals, as well as their needs and deepest desires."

— Steve Jobs

3 – Delving Deep into Customer Experiences

Gaining a deep understanding of the customer's journey is an invaluable exercise that allows you to uncover hidden opportunities and gain a sharper perspective on their problems.

By meticulously mapping out the customer's entire experience, step by step, you can identify pain points and areas for improvement.

Even if you believe you have a clear grasp of the customer's experience, it's still essential to deconstruct it into its constituent parts. This process often leads to surprising insights and the revelation of opportunities that others may have overlooked.

Key Steps:

1. **Identify the Most Valuable Problem:** Prioritize the most valuable (most frequent, most impactful, and most important) problem among the most important customers you've identified.
2. **Conduct In-Depth Interviews:** Engage with at least ten individuals who experience the problem and encourage them to elaborate on their experiences in detail.
3. **Seek Diverse Perspectives:** Avoid relying solely on close friends for these interviews. Seek out individuals from different backgrounds and perspectives to gain a broader understanding of the problem.

4. **Capture Every Detail:** Document every aspect of the problem they describe, including their emotions and frustrations. Consider recording the interviews for future reference.
5. **Reconstruct the Timeline:** If the interviewee doesn't naturally follow a chronological order, ask clarifying questions to piece together the sequence of events.
6. **Evaluate Actions and Difficulty:** List the actions they took to address the problem and assign a difficulty rating (1-10) to each action.
7. **Identify Triggers and Recurrence:** Note the specific events or situations that trigger the problem's recurrence.
8. **Summarize the Experience:** Consolidate the information gathered from multiple interviews into a comprehensive overview of the problem.
9. **Create a Problem-Solving Pool:** Repeat this process for all valuable problems to establish a repository of problem-solving experiences. Use this pool as your primary resource for generating business ideas.
10. **Spot Opportunities:** As you populate the problem-solving pool, identify potential business opportunities that arise from the identified pain points.

Thought-Provoking Questions:

1. What does success mean to you?

This question helps you understand the customer's priorities and aspirations, which can guide your product development and marketing efforts.

2. What is the biggest obstacle preventing you from achieving your definition of success?

This question identifies the most significant problem that the customer faces, which can be the foundation for your business idea.

3. How often have you tried to solve this problem in the past?

This question reveals the frequency of the problem, which can help you assess the market size and potential demand for your solution.

4. What alternative solutions have you tried to solve this problem? Where did you find these alternatives?

This question uncovers the existing solutions in the market and their perceived shortcomings, which can inform your product differentiation strategy.

5. What are the missing components or features that you would like to see in an ideal solution?

This question identifies the unmet needs and expectations of the customer, which can provide valuable insights for product development.

6. Are you currently spending money to address this problem? If so, how much?

This question assesses the customer's willingness to pay for a solution, which can help you determine the pricing strategy for your product or service.

7. *What would an ideal solution to this problem look like for you?*

This question helps you understand the customer's vision of an ideal solution, which can inform your product design and feature development.

8. *How would you feel if someone could solve this problem perfectly for you?*

This question gauges the emotional impact of the problem on the customer, which can be used to craft effective marketing messages that resonate with their frustrations or aspirations.

9. *Do you know anyone else who is facing similar problems to you? Can you introduce me to them?*

This question expands your reach and helps you connect with a broader range of potential customers who share similar pain points.

10. *What are your biggest concerns or hesitations about adopting a new solution to this problem?*

This question identifies potential barriers to adoption and allows you to address them proactively in your product design, marketing messaging, or customer support strategies.

By meticulously following these steps and asking insightful questions, you can uncover hidden opportunities, gain a profound understanding of customer problems, and lay the foundation for innovative business ideas.

Inspiring Business Tales:

✶ **Delta Airlines' Customer Service Evolution (2017):**
Delta Airlines embraced customer journey mapping to revamp its customer service strategy. By identifying pain points and opportunities, Delta implemented changes such as proactive communication during delays and an enhanced baggage tracking system. This customer-centric approach led to improved customer satisfaction and loyalty in the competitive airline industry.

✶ **Fitbit's Health and Wellness Ecosystem (2014):**
Fitbit expanded its focus beyond fitness tracking by mapping the entire health and wellness journey for users. This involved integrating features like sleep tracking, nutrition logging, and community engagement. The comprehensive approach to customer journey mapping transformed Fitbit from a fitness tracker into a holistic health and wellness platform.

✶ **Hilton's Digital Check-In Experience (2016):**
Hilton Hotels leveraged customer journey mapping to optimize the check-in process for guests. Introducing digital check-in and room selection through their mobile app, they minimized wait times and empowered guests with more control over their stay. This innovation highlighted the impact of technology in enhancing the hospitality customer journey.

* **Tesla's Gigafactory Innovation (2014):**
Understanding the limitations of traditional manufacturing processes in producing electric vehicle batteries, Tesla decided to revolutionize its approach. By meticulously mapping the manufacturing journey, Tesla aimed to vertically integrate its battery production. The Gigafactory, established in 2014, became a cornerstone in this strategy, enabling Tesla to control the entire manufacturing process and significantly reduce the cost of electric vehicle production.

> "The customer journey is not just about the steps people take. It's about the emotional experience they have."
>
> — James Gilmore

4 – How to Gain In-Depth Market Insights

Launching a business in an industry you lack knowledge of is akin to diving into the depths without knowing how to swim.

Success in any market hinges on a deep understanding of its intricacies, its players, and its dynamics. If you embark on this journey with a superficial understanding, the path to bankruptcy is all but certain.

Key Steps:

1. Engage with Customers
- *What are the needs, pain points, and expectations of your target customers?*
- *What are their experiences with existing solutions in the market?*
- *How can your product or service address their unmet needs and provide a better experience?*

2. Conduct Surveys
- *Design a simple and comprehensive survey to gather feedback from a diverse range of potential customers.*
- *Utilize digital advertising platforms to expand your reach and collect a wider pool of responses.*
- *Consider conducting phone surveys to gain deeper insights and clarifications.*

3. Delve into Market Research
- *Thoroughly research publicly available studies, articles, presentations, and statistics related to your target market.*
- *Utilize Google Scholar and other research databases to uncover valuable information and trends.*
- *Analyze industry reports, market forecasts, and competitor analyses to gain a comprehensive understanding of the market landscape.*

4. Engage with Online Communities
- *Identify and actively participate in online forums, groups, or communities dedicated to your target market.*
- *Observe trends, identify key concerns and interests of industry participants, and stay abreast of emerging customer preferences.*
- *Network with industry experts, influencers, and potential customers to gain valuable insights and perspectives.*

5. Centralize Your Knowledge
- *Create a centralized Google Drive folder to organize and store your research findings, customer insights, and industry data.*
- *Meticulously categorize and upload new information, ensuring easy access and retrieval.*
- *Regularly review and analyze your accumulated data to identify actionable insights and inform your business decisions.*

Thought-Provoking Questions:

1. Market Size and Growth:

- What is the current and projected sales volume for your target market?
- How large is the current customer base, and what is the projected growth rate?
- What are the key trends shaping the market's growth and evolution?

2. Market Awareness and Understanding:
- How familiar are potential customers with existing solutions and alternatives in the market?
- What are the common misconceptions or gaps in understanding of your target market?
- How can you effectively educate and inform potential customers about the value of your product or service?

3. Customer Purchasing Behavior:
- What are the primary resources used by customers to research potential solutions?
- How do customers evaluate and compare different alternatives before making a purchasing decision?
- What factors ultimately influence the purchasing decisions of your target customers?

4. Competitive Landscape:
- Who are your key competitors, and what are their strengths and weaknesses?
- How does your product or service differentiate from existing solutions in the market?

- What are the perceived gaps and unmet needs that your product or service can address?

5. Customer Feedback and Loyalty:

- How can you effectively gather feedback from customers to continuously improve your product or service?
- What strategies can you implement to build customer loyalty and advocacy?
- How can you create lasting relationships with your customers and foster a sense of community?

Inspiring Business Tales:

✶ **Coca-Cola's New Coke Fiasco (1985):**
Coca-Cola's attempt to reformulate its flagship beverage with "New Coke" without adequate market research is a famous cautionary tale. The negative public reaction and backlash demonstrated the crucial role of understanding consumer preferences through thorough market research. Coca-Cola later reverted to its original formula, highlighting the importance of knowing your market.

✶ **Netflix's Content Strategy (Originals, 2013):**
Netflix's foray into original programming, starting with "House of Cards", was grounded in extensive market research. Analyzing viewer preferences and behavior, Netflix identified a demand for high-quality original content. The success of their original programming validated the importance of data-driven insights in content creation and streaming service strategy.

* **McDonald's All-Day Breakfast (2015):**
McDonald's decision to introduce all-day breakfast was a result of thorough market research. Recognizing changing consumer habits and preferences, McDonald's conducted surveys and tests to gauge the demand for breakfast items throughout the day. The successful implementation of all-day breakfast showcased the brand's responsiveness to consumer needs.

* **Amazon into Grocery (Whole Foods, 2017):**
Amazon's acquisition of Whole Foods was a strategic move backed by market research. Recognizing the increasing demand for organic and healthy food options, Amazon entered the grocery market through this acquisition. The move was informed by insights into consumer preferences and aligned with changing trends in the retail industry.

> *"Understanding your market is the foundation for creating a successful business. Without a deep understanding of your market, you're just guessing."*
>
> *— Michael Porter*

5 – Master the Art of Competitive Intelligence

Understanding your competitors is akin to having a map of the battlefield, illuminating the path to victory.

Just as peach vendors in a neighborhood market meticulously study their rivals' offerings, so too must you delve into the strategies and tactics of your competitors.

In this competitive arena, the interplay of various alternatives shapes the market dynamics. Customers weigh these options carefully, evaluating them against a myriad of criteria. As a product owner, your task is to embark on a reconnaissance mission, exploring the market's offerings and understanding the factors that drive customer choices.

Key Steps:

1. **Market Research:** Conduct a thorough market investigation, identifying all players and their respective products or services.
2. **Product Experience:** Immerse yourself in your competitors' offerings, gaining firsthand experience through trials or demos.
3. **Feature Analysis:** Scrutinize the features and solutions provided by each competitor, noting both common and distinctive elements.

4. **Customer Relations:** Assess your competitors' customer service interactions, reviewing comments and feedback to glean areas for improvement.
5. **Pricing Strategies:** Analyze the pricing strategies employed by your competitors, seeking to understand the rationale behind their pricing decisions.
6. **Business Models:** Deconstruct each competitor's business model, identifying the underlying mechanisms that drive their profitability and success.
7. **Advertising Landscape:** Examine your competitors' advertising campaigns, noting their slogans, imagery, and chosen channels.
8. **Channel Effectiveness:** Evaluate the effectiveness of each advertising channel utilized by your competitors, identifying the most impactful strategies.
9. **Habit and Routine:** Recognize that habits and routines can act as indirect competitors, influencing customer choices. Consider whether Netflix's assertion that their biggest rival is "Customers going out at night or on the weekend, having fun outside" applies to your market.

Thought-Provoking Questions:

Customer Preference:
- *What factors drive customers to choose specific competitors over others?*
- *What unique attributes or offerings attract customers to certain competitors?*
- *How do customer preferences vary across different demographics or market segments?*

Unique Selling Proposition:
- What distinctive features or benefits set your competitors apart from each other?
- How do your competitors communicate their unique selling propositions to customers?
- What gaps or unmet needs exist in the market that your competitors' unique selling propositions fail to address?

Customer Pain Points:
- What common frustrations or complaints do customers express about your competitors?
- What areas of improvement or unmet needs can be identified from customer feedback about your competitors?
- How are your competitors addressing or failing to address the pain points of their target customers?

Geographical Reach:
- In which geographical regions do your competitors have the strongest presence or market share?
- Are there any geographical areas where your competitors are underrepresented or have weaknesses?
- How do your competitors' geographical strategies align with their target customer base and distribution channels?

Organic Search Ranking:
- For what keywords do your competitors consistently rank high in organic search results on Google?
- What content or SEO strategies are your competitors employing to achieve high organic search rankings?

- Are there any opportunities for you to improve your own organic search rankings and visibility by targeting relevant keywords?

Employee Satisfaction:
- What indicators suggest that employees at your competitors' organizations are satisfied or dissatisfied?
- How does employee satisfaction impact customer service, innovation, and overall business performance?
- What can you learn from your competitors' employee satisfaction levels to enhance your own workplace culture and retention strategies?

Customer Decision-Making Criteria:
- What are the most important factors that customers consider when making purchasing decisions in your industry?
- How do your competitors' products or services align with the decision-making criteria of your target customers?
- What unique selling points or value propositions can you emphasize to influence customer decisions in your favor?

Marketing Channel Effectiveness:
- Which marketing channels are most effective in attracting and converting customers for your competitors?
- How do your competitors allocate their marketing budgets across different channels?
- What opportunities exist for you to leverage or adapt your marketing channel strategies to achieve better results?

With competitive analysis, you gain valuable insights into the market landscape, enabling you to craft a differentiated strategy that positions your product or service for success.

Understanding your competitors is not about imitation; it's about leveraging their strengths and learning from their mistakes to forge your own path to victory.

Inspiring Business Tales:

✴ **Google's Surprise to Bing (2009):**
When Microsoft introduced Bing as a competitor to Google's search engine, Google's Competitive intelligence team analyzed Bing's search results. Google suspected that Bing was using data from users' searches on Google to improve its own results. In a strategic move, Google inserted false search results, which later appeared on Bing. This incident highlighted the importance of monitoring and responding to potential misuse of proprietary information.

✴ **Uber's Intelligence on Lyft's Expansion (2014):**
Uber, in a highly competitive ride-sharing market, utilized Competitive intelligence to stay ahead. When rumors circulated about Lyft's plans to expand into certain cities, Uber's team proactively gathered information from job postings, public records, and insider tips. Armed with this intelligence, Uber strategically pre-empted Lyft's expansion, maintaining its strong market presence.

* **Procter & Gamble's Diaper War (1970s - 1980s):**
P&G's Competitive intelligence played a central role in the famous "Diaper War" with Kimberly-Clark. P&G gained insights into Kimberly-Clark's diaper manufacturing processes through a series of dumpster dives, providing valuable information for P&G's product development. This episode emphasizes the lengths companies may go to gather competitive insights.

* **Tesla from Apple (Various Years):**
Tesla, led by Elon Musk, recognized the value of insider information from competitors, particularly Apple. Over the years, Tesla strategically hired key employees from Apple, gaining insights into Apple's approach to design, engineering, and product development. This practice exemplifies how companies can leverage talent acquisition as a form of Competitive intelligence.

> *"It's not just about being better than your competition, it's about being different."*
>
> *— Harvey Mackay*

6 – Building on Proven Concepts

In the realm of business, the pursuit of innovation often leads entrepreneurs to chase groundbreaking ideas.

However, there exists an alternative approach that involves replicating successful concepts that have already proven their worth in the market.

While the allure of an original idea is undeniable, many aspiring entrepreneurs overlook the potential of emulating existing successful businesses.

Consider the inception of social media giants like Twitter and Instagram. Their core concepts - microblogging and photo sharing - were seemingly simple, yet their execution and adaptation to market demands propelled them to global prominence.

The success of these businesses highlights the fact that the idea itself is not always the primary determinant of success. Rather, it is the execution, adaption, and strategic implementation that transform an idea into a thriving enterprise.

Chasing an entirely original idea is akin to playing the lottery - the odds of success are slim, and the path to realization is often fraught with uncertainty. In contrast, replicating proven business models provides a more structured and less risky approach to entrepreneurship.

By focusing on established concepts, entrepreneurs can:

- **Learn from existing models:** Analyze the successes and failures of similar businesses to identify best practices and potential pitfalls.
- **Reduce risk:** Proven business models have already demonstrated market viability, minimizing the risk of failure.
- **Accelerate growth:** By leveraging existing frameworks, entrepreneurs can streamline the development and implementation process.
- **Focus on execution:** With a validated concept, entrepreneurs can direct their energy towards effective execution and market penetration.

Key Steps:

1. **Thorough research:** Conduct in-depth research on your chosen competitors, understanding their strengths, weaknesses, and target market.
2. **Explore emerging trends:** Utilize platforms like Springwise and Trendhunter to identify trending concepts with global potential.
3. **Analyze app store data:** Examine the most popular apps in the Apple and Android app stores to gauge market demand and potential revenue streams.
4. **Seek investment insights:** Review startup investment platforms like Angel.co and Index.co to identify ideas that have attracted professional backing.
5. **Start small:** Begin with a manageable business idea that can generate immediate impact and provide valuable lessons.

6. **Experience the customer journey:** Become a customer of the business you intend to replicate, immersing yourself in their offerings.
7. **Identify areas for improvement:** Scrutinize the existing product or service, seeking opportunities for enhancements and differentiation.
8. **Focus on market expansion:** Prioritize market selection, expanding strategically rather than attempting global conquest prematurely.
9. **Leverage expertise:** Focus on ideas within your area of expertise, minimizing underestimation of challenges and enhancing strategic decision-making.
10. **Embrace iterative development:** Acknowledge that success is not an immediate outcome. Embrace continuous learning, experimentation, and refinement.

Thought-Provoking Questions:

1. **Cultural Sensitivity:** How effectively can you adapt the replicated concept to suit the cultural context of your target market?
2. **Market Size Assessment:** Have you thoroughly analyzed the size and potential of your chosen market, considering factors such as competition, saturation, and growth opportunities?
3. **Learning from Past Failures:** Have you investigated and analyzed failed business ideas in your industry to identify potential pitfalls and areas for improvement?
4. **Side Shop Avoidance:** How will you differentiate your replicated business from existing competitors in the same market?

5. **Intellectual Property Protection:** Have you conducted a thorough assessment of intellectual property rights related to the replicated concept to ensure compliance?
6. **Team Competency:** Does your team possess the necessary expertise, skills, and experience to effectively execute the replicated business model?
7. **Concept Maturity Assessment:** Have you carefully evaluated the maturity of the replicated concept, ensuring it has a demonstrated track record of success and market acceptance?
8. **Cost-Benefit Analysis:** Have you conducted a comprehensive cost-benefit analysis to ensure that the potential rewards of replicating the concept outweigh the associated costs?

Replicating proven business models is a viable and often overlooked path to entrepreneurial success.

By harnessing the insights and strategies of existing businesses, aspiring entrepreneurs can increase their chances of success while minimizing risks and accelerating their journey towards achieving their business goals.

Inspiring Business Tales:

* **Starbucks: Inspired by Italian Coffee Culture**
  - ***Origin:*** *The Starbucks we know today was significantly influenced by Howard Schultz, who, after a trip to Italy, was inspired by the Italian coffee culture. He saw the potential to replicate the experience of Italian espresso bars in the United States.*

- **Adaptation**: Schultz's vision went beyond just selling coffee; it was about recreating the community and ambiance of Italian coffeehouses, fostering a 'third place' between home and work.
- **Success**: This replication and adaptation of the Italian coffee model led to the global success of Starbucks, turning it into the largest coffeehouse chain in the world.

✴ **McDonald's: Standardizing the Fast-Food Concept**
  - **Origin**: Ray Kroc, the man behind McDonald's global expansion, didn't originally come up with the concept of fast food, but he recognized the potential in the McDonald brothers' fast-food restaurant in California.
  - **Adaptation**: Kroc replicated their efficient, assembly-line style food preparation process on a grand scale, maintaining consistency and quality.
  - **Success**: McDonald's became a global phenomenon, largely thanks to Kroc's ability to replicate and scale a successful business model, revolutionizing the fast-food industry.

✴ **Netflix: Adapting the Rental for the Digital Age**
  - **Origin**: Originally, Netflix started as a DVD rental service, similar to the already established Blockbuster. However, they added a unique twist by using the internet for DVD orders and implementing a no-late-fees policy.
  - **Adaptation**: Later, Netflix pivoted and replicated the on-demand streaming model, revolutionizing how people consume media and entertainment.

- **Success**: This adaptation of existing business models led Netflix to become a leader in online streaming, fundamentally changing the entertainment industry.

* **Alibaba: China's Answer to eBay and Amazon**
  - **Origin**: Jack Ma, the founder of Alibaba, was inspired by the successes of eBay and Amazon in the United States.
  - **Adaptation**: He adapted the idea to fit the Chinese market, focusing on connecting Chinese manufacturers with international buyers, and later expanding into e-commerce with platforms like Taobao and Tmall.
  - **Success**: Alibaba became one of the world's largest e-commerce companies, successfully adapting and localizing the online marketplace model for China and beyond.

* **IKEA: Furniture with a Unique Twist**
  - **Origin**: While IKEA did not invent furniture sales, its founder, Ingvar Kamprad, identified a niche in providing affordable, flat-packed, self-assembled furniture.
  - **Adaptation**: IKEA took the basic idea of selling furniture and combined it with an efficient, cost-effective model that appealed to a wide demographic looking for affordable, stylish options.
  - **Success**: This approach revolutionized the furniture industry, making IKEA the world's largest furniture retailer with a unique brand identity.

- **Xiaomi: Apple's Design, Tailoring for China**
  - *Origin*: Xiaomi, often referred to as the 'Apple of China', initially drew heavy inspiration from Apple in terms of product design and marketing.
  - *Adaptation*: They adapted this model to the Chinese market, focusing on high-quality, affordable smartphones with a user-centric, online-only sales model.
  - *Success*: Xiaomi quickly gained a massive following, becoming one of the leading smartphone manufacturers globally by combining Apple's design ethos with affordability and local market understanding.

- **Instagram: Elevating the Photo-Sharing Experience**
  - *Origin*: While photo sharing wasn't a new concept with platforms like Flickr in existence, Instagram's founders saw an opportunity to enhance this experience on mobile devices.
  - *Adaptation*: They focused on a mobile-first, user-friendly interface with unique filters and social networking features, differentiating Instagram from existing photo-sharing websites.
  - *Success*: Instagram quickly became hugely popular, especially among younger audiences, leading to its acquisition by Facebook and cementing its status as a key player in social media.

"Great people actually understand at a deeper level what makes something great and then build on the shoulders of that and build something even more marvelous and take it further"

– Steve Jobs

7 – The Acquisition Advantage

In the pursuit of success, the path often taken is that of entrepreneurship, building an enterprise from the ground up.

However, this is not the only route to achieving your goals. Just as innovation isn't always about groundbreaking ideas, establishing a successful business doesn't always necessitate starting from scratch.

Acquiring an existing business offers a compelling alternative, providing a ready-made foundation for your entrepreneurial aspirations.

By carefully navigating the acquisition process, you can leverage the existing infrastructure, customer base, and brand reputation of an established enterprise, potentially accelerating your path to success.

Key Steps:

1. **Customer Experience Evaluation:** Before committing to a purchase, immerse yourself in the business as a customer. Assess the customer experience firsthand to ensure that the business's positive attributes extend beyond mere paper-based financials. Identifying potential shortcomings can strengthen your bargaining position during negotiations.
2. **Sales Experience Simulation:** To fully grasp the business's operations, step into the shoes of a

salesperson. Try selling the product or service yourself. If you encounter difficulties, it may indicate a need for further evaluation before committing to the acquisition.

3. **Leveraging External Resources:** Acquiring a business doesn't require you to solely rely on your own funds. If you believe in the business's potential, consider seeking investment from individuals or organizations with the necessary capital. This can reduce your financial risk while allowing you to retain a significant ownership stake.
4. **Franchise/Dealership Opportunities:** Explore franchise or dealership opportunities, which offer established business models with brand recognition and support systems. This can be a suitable option if you seek a structured approach to entrepreneurship.
5. **Demonstrating Value Proposition:** When approaching the business owner, articulate the value you bring to the table beyond financial resources. Highlight your expertise, growth plans, and how your involvement will enhance the business's success.
6. **Due Diligence:** Engage an independent institution to conduct a thorough assessment of the business's financial health, legal standing, and overall value. This due diligence process will provide you with critical insights to inform your decision-making.
7. **Financing Options:** If your personal funds are insufficient, explore financing options from banks or other lending institutions. Secure a loan with favorable terms to bridge the funding gap.
8. **Financial Analysis:** Prepare a comprehensive financial plan that encompasses all income and expense items, both visible and invisible, immediate and deferred.

9. **Transition Planning:** Develop a transition plan that addresses employee integration, technology migration, and operational continuity following the acquisition.
10. **Expert Guidance:** Seek the counsel of experienced professionals specializing in business acquisitions. Their expertise can guide you through the complexities of the acquisition process and safeguard your interests.

Thought-Provoking Questions:

Availability for Sale
- *Is the business actually for sale?*
- *Has the owner made a firm decision to sell?*
- *Are there any contingencies or obstacles that could prevent the sale from going through?*

Business Fundamentals
- *Are the business's fundamentals strong?*
- *Does the business have a proven track record of success?*
- *Is the business well-positioned for growth in the future?*
- *Will acquiring the business save you time and effort, or will you need to do a lot of work from scratch?*

Non-Monetary Value Creation
- *What non-monetary value can you bring to the business?*
- *Can you offer your expertise, skills, or experience to improve the business?*
- *Do you have a network of contacts that could be beneficial to the business?*

Legal Documentation
- *Do you have access to all relevant legal documents pertaining to the business's past and future operations?*

- *Have you reviewed the business's financial statements, tax returns, and legal contracts?*
- *Are there any potential legal issues that could arise post-acquisition?*

Asset Clarity
- *What exactly are you buying?*
- *Are fixtures, licenses, patents, and other intangible assets included in the sale?*
- *Is there a clear understanding of the business's intellectual property rights?*

Legal and Financial Encumbrances
- *Are there any potential tax liabilities that could arise post-acquisition?*
- *Are there any debts or other financial obligations that will be transferred to you as the new owner?*
- *Have you received written assurances from the seller regarding any potential legal or financial issues?*

Reputation Assessment
- *What is the company's reputation, past and present?*
- *Has the company been involved in any negative incidents or legal disputes?*
- *What do online customer reviews say about the company?*

Key Employee Retention
- *Are any critical employees planning to leave the company after the acquisition?*
- *Have you identified any potential risks associated with employee turnover?*
- *What steps can you take to retain key employees and maintain continuity of operations?*

Information Access
- *Do you have access to all necessary information, passwords, and confidential files to effectively manage the business?*
- *Have you established a clear process for transitioning control of the business to you as the new owner?*
- *Are there any potential risks associated with data security or intellectual property protection?*

Inspiring Business Tales:

* **Disney's Acquisition of Pixar (2006)**
    - ***Background***: *The Walt Disney Company acquired Pixar Animation Studios for approximately $7.4 billion.*
    - ***Impact***: *This acquisition brought together Disney's historic brand and Pixar's cutting-edge animation technology and creative storytelling. It revitalized Disney's animation division and led to a series of blockbuster films, including "Toy Story 3," "Up," and "Inside Out."*
    - ***Significance***: *The acquisition demonstrated the power of combining strong, creative content with established branding and distribution channels.*

* **Google's Purchase of Android (2005)**
    - ***Background***: *Google acquired a then little-known mobile software company, Android Inc., for an estimated $50 million.*
    - ***Impact***: *Android went on to become the foundation for Google's mobile operating system, which is now used in over 2.5 billion devices globally.*
    - ***Significance***: *The acquisition was a strategic move that allowed Google to enter and eventually dominate the*

mobile operating system market, a key area for the company's long-term growth.

* **Facebook Acquiring Instagram (2012)**
  * *Background*: Facebook acquired Instagram for about $1 billion, a move that was initially met with skepticism.
  * *Impact*: Instagram's user base skyrocketed under Facebook's ownership, and it became a significant platform for digital marketing, especially among younger demographics.
  * *Significance*: This acquisition not only helped Facebook capture a younger audience but also solidified its position in the social media landscape, especially in mobile.

* **Walmart's Acquisition of jet.com (2016)**
  * *Background*: Walmart acquired Jet.com for around $3.3 billion to bolster its e-commerce presence.
  * *Impact*: The acquisition helped Walmart accelerate its online growth and compete more effectively with Amazon.
  * *Significance*: This deal represented a strategic shift for Walmart, showcasing its recognition of the growing importance of e-commerce and its commitment to investing in this area.

* **Salesforce's Acquisition of Slack (2020)**
  * *Background*: Salesforce, a leader in CRM software, announced the acquisition of Slack Technologies, Inc., for approximately $27.7 billion.
  * *Impact*: The acquisition aimed to integrate Slack's communication platform with Salesforce's cloud-based

software suite, enhancing enterprise collaboration and productivity.
- **Significance**: The acquisition was a strategic move to bolster Salesforce's offerings in an increasingly digital and remote work environment, positioning it to better compete with rivals like Microsoft.

> *"It's far better to buy a wonderful company at a fair price than a fair company at a wonderful price."*
>
> *— Warren Buffett*

8 – How to Generate Business Ideas that Sell

In the fast-paced world of business, innovation is the key to survival and success.

However, many individuals struggle to generate fresh ideas, often feeling like they're running on empty when it comes to creativity.

We are here to dispel this notion and provide a practical guide to unlocking your creative potential.

Key Steps:

Step 1: Define the Problem or Opportunity
Before embarking on the ideation process, it's crucial to clearly define the problem or opportunity you're addressing. This will help focus your efforts and ensure that your ideas are relevant and aligned with the specific challenge at hand.

Step 2: Embrace a Beginner's Mind
Approach the problem with a fresh perspective, setting aside any preconceived notions or assumptions. This helps open your mind to new possibilities and uncover unconventional solutions.

**Step 3: Apply the "It's Alright" Filter

Evaluate your ideas against the "It's alright" filter. If you can imagine life without your proposed product or service, it's unlikely to be truly transformative. Aim for ideas that create a noticeable void in people's lives.

Step 4: Cultivate an Idea-Generating Ecosystem

Surround yourself with a community of creative individuals who share your passion for innovation. Engage in regular brainstorming sessions and discussions to stimulate fresh ideas.

Step 5: Engage with Diverse Perspectives

Seek out conversations with people from different backgrounds and experiences. Their unique perspectives can provide valuable insights and challenge your assumptions.

Step 6: Explore Unfamiliar Domains

Venture beyond your industry and explore books, articles, and concepts from other fields. This exposure to diverse ideas can spark unexpected connections and lead to breakthrough solutions.

Step 7: Stay Abreast of Trends

Utilize online resources like Google Trends and Springwise to identify emerging trends and consumer behaviors. These insights can inform your ideation process and help you anticipate future needs.

Step 8: Delve into Sector Research

Keep up-to-date with industry-specific research reports and publications. This knowledge can reveal untapped opportunities and inform your understanding of the competitive landscape.

Step 9: Identify Human Inefficiencies

Observe people's daily routines and identify areas where they struggle or experience inefficiencies. Consider how you can develop solutions to enhance their productivity and well-being.

Step 10: Bend the Rules of Innovation

Challenge conventional thinking by applying techniques like inversion, combination, and simplification. These approaches can lead to disruptive and game-changing ideas.

Thought-Provoking Questions:

1. Can it be done cheaper?
2. Can it be done faster?
3. Can it be done with better quality?
4. Can it be done easier?
5. Can it be done more efficiently?
6. Can it be made more durable?
7. Envision a solution that is 100 times better than current options.
8. Did you try apply creative ideas or models from other industries to your sector.
9. Did you try to adapt an old idea to the modern context.
10. Did you eliminate the concept of "impossible" and brainstorm solutions that defy conventional thinking.

By embracing these strategies and cultivating a growth mindset, you can unlock your creative potential and generate innovative ideas that drive success. Creativity is not a fixed trait but a skill that can be developed and nurtured through consistent practice and an open mind.

Inspiring Business Tales:

* **Richard Branson and Virgin Group**

Richard Branson's journey with Virgin Records began unexpectedly when he launched a magazine called "Student" at 16. To fund the magazine, he started a mail-order record business. He then progressed to opening a record shop, a recording studio, and finally the record label itself. Branson's creative approach to business, focusing on areas where customer service was poor, led him to disrupt various industries, from music to airlines, with the Virgin brand.

* **Howard Schultz and Starbucks**

Howard Schultz's trip to Italy in the 1980s inspired him to transform Starbucks, then a small coffee bean store, into a coffee shop model focused on the experience of coffee drinking, rather than just the sale of coffee beans. Schultz was inspired by the Italian coffee culture and envisioned a third place between work and home for people to enjoy coffee and community. This led to the reimagining of Starbucks into a global coffeehouse chain.

* **Salvador Dalí's Surreal Dream Technique**

Salvador Dalí, the famous surrealist artist, used a peculiar method to gather ideas. He would sit with a spoon in his hand and relax into a semi-sleep state. As he dozed off, the spoon would drop, waking him and allowing him to capture the surreal images of his dreams. This technique, known as 'slumber with a key,' was Dalí's way of tapping into his subconscious mind, leading to the dreamlike, surreal imagery in his artwork.

* **Pablo Picasso and Cubism**
Picasso's creative breakthrough came with the development of Cubism, influenced by African and Iberian art. He was continually seeking to challenge the norms of the art world. His exploration and willingness to embrace different cultural art forms led to a groundbreaking new style, forever changing the landscape of modern art.

* **J.K. Rowling and the Harry Potter Series**
J.K. Rowling's idea for the Harry Potter series came to her during a train journey from Manchester to London. She didn't have a pen and was too shy to ask for one, so she spent the next four hours conceptualizing the story in her mind. This moment of forced contemplation without immediate writing allowed her imagination to run, leading to one of the most successful book series in history.

> *"Creativity is a wild mind and a disciplined eye."*
>
> *— Dorothy Parker*

9 – Taming the Idea Jungle: Best Idea to Pursue?

In the bustling realm of ideas, we often find ourselves overwhelmed by a multitude of promising concepts.

This dilemma of choosing the right idea to pursue can be a daunting one, especially when we've nurtured each idea like our own child.

However, by adopting a structured and thoughtful approach, we can effectively select the idea that holds the greatest potential for success.

Key Steps:

Step 1: Self-Commitment
Before embarking on the evaluation process, make a solemn commitment to yourself. Pledge to dedicate your full attention and effort to nurturing the chosen idea, ensuring its success. Remember, this commitment is an investment in your future and a testament to your belief in your abilities.

Step 2: Defining Unconsidered Aspects
Scrutinize each idea, identifying any potential aspects that may not have been fully explored. This could involve market research, technical feasibility assessments, or financial projections. By addressing these unknowns, you

gain a more comprehensive understanding of each idea's potential.

Step 3: Crafting an Idea Comparison Chart

Construct a table to compare and contrast your ideas based on a set of predetermined criteria. These criteria could include:

- **Innovation:** Does the idea introduce a novel technical solution?
- **Sustainable Singularity:** How difficult would it be for others to replicate your idea?
- **Income Potential:** What level of revenue could the idea generate?
- **Target Market:** How many potential customers are there for this product or service?
- **Investor Appeal:** How attractive would the idea be to potential investors?
- **Cost-Effectiveness:** How much capital is required to implement the idea?
- **Expertise Requirements:** What level of expertise do you possess to execute the idea?

Step 4: Assigning Weighted Scores

Not all criteria carry equal weight. Assign a weighting factor to each criterion, reflecting its relative importance to you. For instance, if income generation is your top priority, the idea with the highest revenue potential should receive a higher weighting.

Step 5: Seeking External Perspectives

Gather feedback from trusted colleagues or mentors, asking them to evaluate each idea based on the comparison chart. Having at least five impartial assessments provides valuable insights and helps minimize personal biases.

Thought-Provoking Questions:

Delve deeper into each idea by asking yourself these introspective questions:

1. **Passion and Pride:** Which idea excites you the most? Which one would you be most proud to implement?
2. **Customer Value:** Is the idea a "vitamin" (essential for customers) or a "painkiller" (irreplaceable solution)? Prioritize painkillers.
3. **Time Commitment:** Which idea requires the least time commitment for success and management?
4. **Motivation and Attention:** Which idea demands the most attention? Are you prepared to provide it?
5. **Legal and Regulatory Compliance:** Are there any legal or regulatory hurdles associated with the idea?
6. **Personal Integrity:** Would implementing the idea compromise your values or reputation?
7. **Global Potential:** Which idea has the greatest potential to scale globally?
8. **Market Trends:** Is the industry the idea operates in growing or declining? Avoid declining markets.
9. **Competitive Landscape:** How likely are you to face fierce competition for this idea?
10. **Existing Commitments:** How would pursuing this new idea impact your existing projects or business?

By carefully evaluating your ideas, seeking external perspectives, and reflecting on your personal aspirations, you can confidently identify the idea with the highest potential for success. Remember, selecting the right idea is not just about maximizing profits; it's about pursuing a venture that aligns with your values, ignites your passion, and contributes positively to the world.

Inspiring Business Tales:

* **Google's Focus on Search Engine Optimization**
While Google started as just another search engine among many, its focus on improving and perfecting search engine algorithms set it apart. Google's emphasis on delivering the best possible search experience made it the dominant search engine, illustrating the power of focusing on a core idea and continuously refining it.

* **Dyson's Bagless Vacuum Cleaner**
James Dyson pursued the development of a bagless vacuum cleaner, working on over 5,000 prototypes before finding success. Despite numerous failures and skepticism, Dyson's persistence paid off. His invention of the bagless vacuum cleaner transformed the home appliance market and established the Dyson brand as a symbol of innovation.

* **SpaceX's Reusable Rockets**
Elon Musk's space exploration company, SpaceX, pursued the ambitious idea of creating reusable rockets, a concept that many in the industry viewed as impractical or impossible. The successful development and landing of reusable rockets, like the Falcon 9, not only reduced the cost of space travel but also positioned SpaceX as a groundbreaking leader in the industry.

* **LinkedIn's Professional Networking Focus**

LinkedIn, co-founded by Reid Hoffman, chose to differentiate itself from other social networks by focusing exclusively on professional networking. This focus on connecting professionals and creating a platform for career networking and recruitment positioned LinkedIn as the go-to social network for the professional world.

> **"People think focus means saying yes to the thing you've got to focus on. But that's not what it means at all.**
>
> **It means saying no to the hundred other good ideas that there are. You have to pick carefully. I'm actually as proud of the things we haven't done as the things I have done. Innovation is saying no to 1,000 things."**
>
> **— Steve Jobs**

Design Revenue-Generating Business Model

While a groundbreaking business idea is the foundation for success, it's the underlying commercial model that breathes life into that idea and transforms it into a profitable enterprise.

Many entrepreneurs mistakenly believe that a great idea alone is sufficient for success, assuming that a revenue-generating model will magically emerge.

However, this passive approach is not only unrealistic but also disregards the critical role of a well-defined business model in guiding the product's journey from conception to market dominance.

The misconception that a good business idea will somehow generate revenue is akin to relying on fate to determine the product's financial outcome.

This lack of control over the product's monetization strategy can be detrimental to its long-term sustainability. Instead, entrepreneurs should actively seek out and implement innovative business models that align with the product's value proposition and target audience.

While traditional commercial models like advertising, sponsorship, and direct sales to brands are often the first options that come to mind, there exists a vast array of creative and unconventional models waiting to be explored. These models, when carefully tailored to the product's unique characteristics and market dynamics, can unlock new revenue streams and propel the business towards financial success.

In essence, a well-crafted business model is the bridge that connects a creative idea to its potential customers.

It outlines the strategies and mechanisms by which the product's value is captured and translated into financial gains. With a proactive approach to developing a robust business model, entrepreneurs can transform their creative spark into a profitable venture that not only generates revenue but also creates sustainable value for all stakeholders.

1 – Differentiate to Dominate

In today's competitive market, it's crucial to differentiate your product to capture customer attention and drive sales.

People don't simply buy products or services; they invest in solutions that enhance their lives. They seek products that address their specific needs, problems, and aspirations.

Before delving into product development, it's essential to understand the psychology behind consumer behavior. People generally turn to external solutions only when their own efforts to resolve an issue have failed. They've exhausted their options and are seeking an effective remedy.

Differentiation boils down to offering something unique and valuable that resonates with your target audience. Your product should stand out from the crowd, addressing a significant need for a substantial number of customers. Ideally, it should provide a solution that surpasses existing alternatives.

Here are three key factors to consider when evaluating your product's potential for differentiation:

- **Solves a Critical Need:** Your product should address a pressing and widespread problem that affects a large population.

- **Unique Solution:** Your product should offer a novel and innovative approach to solving the problem, something that hasn't been done before.
- **Exceptional Performance:** Your product should deliver exceptional performance, exceeding the functionality and effectiveness of existing solutions.

While innovation is admirable, it's important to acknowledge the rarity of truly groundbreaking ideas. The vast majority of business ideas fall into the realm of incremental improvements.

If your product has an **unfair advantage** that gives your business a significant edge. This difference can be based on a variety of factors, including:

- **Proprietary technology:** Developing a unique and valuable technology that provides a significant performance or efficiency advantage. Protect your intellectual property: Patent it.
- **Exclusive access to resources:** Securing access to raw materials, distribution channels, or other resources that competitors cannot easily obtain.
- **Unmatched expertise:** Building a team with deep domain knowledge and experience that allows you to solve problems and innovate in ways that others cannot.
- **Superior customer experience:** Creating a seamless and delightful customer experience that builds loyalty and advocacy.
- **Disruptive business model:** Redefining the industry norms by offering a completely different way of doing business.

Key Steps:

Here are practical steps to differentiate your product in the market:

1. **Radical Solutions:** Seek radical solutions to the most critical problems faced by your target users.
2. **Address Competitor Weaknesses:** Identify and capitalize on the shortcomings of your competitors. Show customers that you understand their pain points and offer superior solutions.
3. **Design and Aesthetics:** Beyond functionality, prioritize user experience, design, aesthetics, and attention to detail.
4. **Enhanced Features:** Offer more or improved features compared to existing products.
5. **Customization:** Cater to specific customer segments by tailoring your product to their unique needs.
6. **Personalization:** Allow users to customize the product to suit their individual preferences and usage patterns.
7. **Streamlined Services:** Simplify and expedite the ordering, delivery, installation, and support processes.
8. **Exceptional Customer Service:** Provide exceptional customer support that exceeds expectations and fosters customer loyalty.
9. **Quantity and Size:** Differentiate by offering more than your competitors, considering cost optimization.
10. **Challenging Industry Norms:** Question industry norms and identify opportunities to disrupt or improve upon established practices.

Thought-Provoking Questions:

1. What are the most pressing pain points, unmet needs, and frustrations of your target customers?
- Conduct deep customer research to uncover hidden needs and identify opportunities for innovation.
- Engage in customer interviews, surveys, and focus groups to gather insights into their pain points and aspirations.
- Analyze customer reviews and social media feedback to understand their perceptions of your product and its competitors.

2. How are your competitors addressing these needs and what are their shortcomings?
- Conduct a thorough competitor analysis to identify their strengths, weaknesses, and market positioning.
- Evaluate their product offerings, pricing strategies, and marketing campaigns to understand their competitive advantage.
- Identify areas where your competitors are falling short and capitalize on these gaps to differentiate your product.

3. What unique value proposition can your product offer that sets it apart from the competition?
- Clearly articulate the unique value proposition that your product delivers to its users.
- Highlight the key features and benefits that address your target customers' specific needs and pain points.
- Demonstrate how your product solves problems in a way that is superior to existing alternatives.

4. *How can you leverage emerging technologies or trends to create innovative solutions?*
- Stay up-to-date on the latest advancements in technology and explore their potential applications.
- Consider how emerging technologies can enhance your product's functionality, efficiency, or user experience.
- Seek partnerships with technology companies to develop innovative solutions that disrupt the market.

5. *How can you tailor your product to the specific needs and preferences of different customer segments?*
- Segment your target market into distinct groups based on their demographics, needs, and usage patterns.
- Develop customized features, variations, or pricing strategies to cater to the unique needs of each segment.
- Personalize the user experience to make your product more relevant and engaging for each individual customer.

6. *How can you create a seamless and delightful customer experience throughout the entire customer journey?*
- Simplify and streamline the customer journey, from initial awareness to post-purchase interactions.
- Provide exceptional customer service that is responsive, helpful, and exceeds expectations.
- Design a user-friendly interface and provide intuitive navigation to enhance the overall customer experience.

7. *How can you leverage storytelling and emotional connection to build brand loyalty and advocacy?*
- Create a compelling brand narrative that resonates with your target audience's values and aspirations.

- Communicate your brand's story through authentic and engaging content that evokes emotion and builds a connection.
- Encourage customer participation and feedback to foster a sense of community and loyalty.

8. How can you utilize data and analytics to gain insights and drive product improvements?

- Collect and analyze customer data to understand their usage patterns, preferences, and satisfaction levels.
- Identify areas for product improvement and prioritize features based on user feedback and data insights.
- Use data-driven decision-making to optimize your product development and marketing strategies.

9. How can you stay ahead of the curve and adapt to changing market trends and customer expectations?

- Continuously monitor industry trends, competitor activities, and emerging technologies.
- Gather real-time feedback from customers to identify emerging needs and market shifts.
- Adopt a culture of innovation and experimentation to continuously test and refine your product offerings.

10. How can you measure the effectiveness of your differentiation strategy and track its impact on business outcomes?

- Establish clear metrics to track key performance indicators (KPIs) related to product differentiation.
- Monitor customer acquisition, retention, and satisfaction rates to assess the impact of your differentiation strategy.

- Analyze sales data and market share to evaluate the effectiveness of your product positioning and pricing strategy.

In a competitive marketplace, differentiation is the key to success. By understanding customer needs, prioritizing unique solutions, and implementing effective differentiation strategies, you can attract customers, foster loyalty, and achieve sustainable growth.

Inspiring Business Tales:

* **Nespresso's Business Model: Affordable Machines and Profitable Capsules**
    - **Strategy**: Nespresso, a division of the Nestlé Group, adopted a unique business model by offering its espresso machines at a relatively affordable price point.
    - **Revenue Focus**: The primary profit driver for Nespresso is not the machines themselves but the sale of proprietary coffee capsules, which are required to operate the machines.
    - **Impact**: This approach allows easy entry for consumers into the Nespresso ecosystem, where the ongoing purchase of capsules generates consistent revenue for the company.
    - **Significance**: Nespresso's model is a classic example of the razor-and-blades business strategy, where the initial product is sold at a low price to boost the sale of complementary consumable goods.

* **Blue Apron's Meal Kit Delivery Service**

Blue Apron entered the food industry with a model of delivering meal kits with pre-portioned ingredients and recipes to customers' doors. By simplifying meal preparation and reducing food waste, Blue Apron appealed to busy consumers looking for convenient cooking solutions, differentiating itself in the burgeoning food delivery market.

✳ **Duolingo's Gamification of Language Learning**
Duolingo entered the language learning market with a free, app-based model that used gamification to make learning a new language more engaging and accessible. This unique approach, combined with adaptive learning technology, made Duolingo a popular tool for language learners worldwide, differentiating it from more traditional language learning methods.

✳ **Slack's Redefinition of Workplace Communication**
Slack transformed workplace communication by offering a platform that consolidated various forms of communication (like email, instant messaging, and file sharing) into one seamless interface. By focusing on reducing email overload and improving team collaboration, Slack offered a fresh approach to communication in the workplace, quickly gaining popularity among businesses.

✳ **Lush Cosmetics' Ethical and Fresh Approach**
Lush Cosmetics set itself apart in the beauty industry with a focus on fresh, handmade, and ethically sourced products, including a strong stance against animal testing. This commitment to ethical production and natural ingredients, combined with a unique in-store experience, established Lush as a distinct and conscientious brand in the crowded cosmetics market.

✸ TOMS Shoes' One-for-One Model

TOMS Shoes, founded by Blake Mycoskie, introduced a unique business model where for every pair of shoes sold, a pair would be donated to a child in need. This one-for-one model not only set TOMS apart from traditional footwear companies but also introduced social entrepreneurship into the mainstream, creating a trend of companies with integrated social causes.

> **"In every company, differentiation is never more important than it is in times of trouble, and that's the time when everyone tends to go to the well and equalize rather than differentiate."**
>
> **— Jack Welch**

2 – Craft Your Business Model

The notion that a brilliant idea can flourish without a viable commercial strategy is nothing short of a fallacy.

Every company that successfully delivers a solution to the market inevitably receives something of value in return from its customers. This is the fundamental principle of business.

The exchange of value can manifest in various forms, often monetary but not always. Regardless of the form, every enterprise operating in the market adheres to a strategic plan, commonly known as a business model.

Steve Blank aptly defines a startup as a collective of individuals united in the pursuit of a scalable and replicable business model.

Without the ability to scale and expand, startups inevitably face the prospect of failure. Growth is inextricably linked to the startup's monthly revenue generation. The absence of revenue necessitates external funding for sustainability.

Consider the expenses, the money spent on salaries, office rent, and various operational costs. If, after accounting for these expenses, a surplus remains, then one can genuinely claim to be running a business.

The philosophy of "launch first, monetize later" is a gamble, with a success probability of one in a million. Twitter, Facebook, and Instagram are rare examples of businesses that have thrived on this approach. However, their "user-centric" strategy is not a universally applicable formula for success.

Key Steps:

1. **Clearly Define Your Solution:** Distinctly articulate the solution you offer to the market. (See: Make a Difference)
2. **Analyze Competitor Models:** Scrutinize the business models employed by competitors offering similar solutions. (See: Scan Your Competitors)
3. **Uncover Customer Needs:** Delve into customer desires beyond what existing solutions offer. (See: Discover Your Customer)
4. **Embrace Model Flexibility:** A unique commercial model is not a prerequisite. Experiment with multiple models simultaneously or combine existing models.
5. **Model-Product Fit:** Tailor your commercial model to align seamlessly with your product's unique characteristics.

Every successful business hinges on a well-defined commercial model, a strategic plan that outlines how your company will generate revenue and capture value.

Selecting the right model is crucial for aligning your product or service with customer needs and achieving sustainable growth.

Merchant Model:
- Concept: This model involves purchasing products at a low cost from manufacturers and selling them to customers with a markup.
- Example: Retailers like Walmart and Target operate under this model.

Manufacturer Model:
- Concept: Companies acquire raw materials and transform them into finished products at a higher cost, adding value through the manufacturing process.
- Example: Automobile manufacturers like Toyota and Honda exemplify this model.

Subscription Model:
- Concept: Customers pay a recurring fee for ongoing access to a product or service.
- Example: Subscription services like Netflix and Spotify utilize this model.

Pay-As-You-Go Model:
- Concept: Customers are charged based on their usage of a product or service.
- Example: Utility companies often employ this model for electricity and water consumption.

Tiered Pricing Model:
- Concept: Customers are offered different pricing packages based on their usage preferences, quantity, or frequency.
- Example: Mobile carriers often provide tiered plans for varying data and call usage.

Freemium Model:
- Concept: Basic features of a product or service are offered for free, while premium features require a paid subscription.
- Example: LinkedIn and Dropbox follow this model.

Trial Model:
- Concept: Customers can access a product or service with all its features for a limited period before deciding to purchase it.
- Example: Software companies often offer free trials to attract new users.

Rental Model:
- Concept: Customers gain temporary access to high-value products at a fraction of the purchase price.
- Example: Car rental companies operate under this model.

Value-Based Pricing:
- Concept: Customers pay a lower price for products or services with reduced features or service quality.
- Example: Discount airlines often offer lower fares with fewer amenities.

Advertising Model:
- Concept: Users receive a free product or service in exchange for viewing advertisements.
- Example: Social media platforms like Facebook and YouTube rely on advertising revenue.

Intermediary Model:

- Concept: A platform connects buyers and sellers, earning a commission on transactions.
- Example: E-commerce marketplaces like Amazon and eBay utilize this model.

Disintermediation Model:
- Concept: A company eliminates intermediaries and sells directly to customers, reducing costs and potentially offering lower prices.
- Example: Dell Computer revolutionized the PC industry by selling directly to consumers.

Affiliate Marketing Model:
- Concept: Affiliates earn commissions by promoting a company's products or services to their audience.
- Example: Many online retailers use affiliate marketing to expand their reach.

Open-Source Model:
- Concept: The core product is offered freely, and the company generates revenue by providing support, customization, or enterprise-level solutions.
- Example: Linux is a widely used open-source operating system.

Open Data Model:
- Concept: Data is collected and made publicly available, and the company generates revenue through donations or by providing value-added services.
- Example: OpenStreetMap is an open-source collaborative mapping project.

Membership Model:

- Concept: Organizations offer free membership with the goal of attracting paid memberships from individuals or institutions.
- Example: Professional associations often follow this model.

Add-On Model:
- Concept: A free or low-cost product is complemented by an additional product or service that is sold separately.
- Example: Razor manufacturers often sell replacement blades for their razors.

Invisible Consumption Model:
- Concept: A product is sold at a discounted price, and the company generates revenue from the sale of essential consumables or accessories.
- Example: Printer manufacturers often sell printers at low prices and make profits from selling ink cartridges.

Reverse Auction Model:
- Concept: Buyers submit bids for a product or service, and the seller awards the contract to the highest bidder.
- Example: Government procurement often involves reverse auctions.

Forward Auction Model:
- Concept: Sellers submit bids for a product or service, and the buyer awards the contract to the lowest bidder.
- Example: Online auction platforms like eBay utilize forward auctions.

Dues Model:

- Concept: Organizations collect membership fees from individuals or institutions to support their activities.
- Example: Labor unions often charge dues to their members.

Thought-Provoking Questions:

1. *What value proposition does your business model offer to customers?*
    - Clearly articulate the unique value proposition that your business model provides to target customers.
    - Highlight how your solution addresses customer needs, solves their problems, and provides them with tangible benefits.
    - Differentiate your value proposition from existing alternatives and emphasize its competitive edge.

2. *What are the key customer segments that your business model targets?*
    - Identify specific customer segments that represent your ideal customers.
    - Understand the unique needs, preferences, and behaviors of each customer segment.
    - Tailor your value proposition, marketing strategies, and customer experience to resonate with each segment.

3. *What are the key channels and partnerships that your business model leverages?*
    - Identify the most effective channels for reaching, engaging, and acquiring customers within each target segment.

- Consider online platforms, social media, partnerships, referral programs, and offline channels.
- Establish strategic partnerships that complement your business model and provide access to valuable resources.

4. *What are the key revenue streams that your business model generates?*
    - Explore various revenue streams that align with your value proposition and target market.
    - Consider direct sales, subscriptions, advertising, affiliate marketing, or other monetization strategies.
    - Evaluate the profitability and sustainability of each revenue stream and identify potential growth opportunities.

5. *What are the key resources and activities required to execute your business model?*
    - Identify the critical resources and activities that are essential for delivering your value proposition.
    - Consider physical assets, intellectual property, technological infrastructure, human capital, and key processes.
    - Optimize resource allocation and streamline activities to enhance efficiency and reduce costs.

6. *What are the key partnerships and supplier relationships that your business model relies on?*
    - Establish strategic partnerships that provide access to valuable resources, expertise, and market reach.

- Develop mutually beneficial relationships with suppliers to ensure reliable access to high-quality products or services.
- Leverage partnerships to enhance your business capabilities and reduce operational risks.

7. What are the key cost structures associated with your business model?
   - Develop a detailed cost structure that includes all the expenses associated with running your business.
   - Consider direct costs, such as production, marketing, and sales, as well as overhead costs.
   - Identify areas for cost optimization and efficiency improvements to enhance profitability.

8. What are the key metrics for measuring the success of your business model?
   - Establish key performance indicators (KPIs) that align with your business objectives and track progress.
   - Consider metrics such as customer acquisition cost, customer lifetime value, revenue growth, profit margins, and customer satisfaction.
   - Use data-driven insights to make informed decisions, optimize your business model, and achieve sustainable growth.

9. How will you test and iterate on your business model assumptions?
   - Develop a process for testing and validating your business model assumptions and hypotheses.

- Utilize lean startup principles to create prototypes, gather feedback, and refine your value proposition and strategy.
- Be agile and adaptable, willing to pivot or adjust your business model based on market insights and customer response.

10. How will you adapt your business model to evolving market conditions and customer needs?
    - Continuously monitor industry trends, technological advancements, and competitor strategies.
    - Be prepared to adapt your business model to stay relevant, maintain a competitive edge, and seize new opportunities.
    - Embrace innovation and explore new ways to enhance customer value, expand your reach, and achieve long-term success.

In essence, a business model serves as the blueprint for value creation and capture, ensuring that your enterprise not only solves a problem but also generates sustainable revenue, paving the way for long-term success.

Inspiring Business Tales:

* **Spotify: Democratizing Music Streaming with the Subscription Model**

Spotify capitalized on the subscription model to transform the music industry, providing users with on-demand access to an extensive music library for a monthly fee. This model addressed the issue of music piracy and provided a sustainable revenue stream for artists and record labels.

These examples demonstrate how choosing the right business model can be a crucial factor in a company's success. By aligning the business model with the nature of the product and the needs of the market, companies can establish a competitive advantage, achieve sustainable growth, and revolutionize their respective industries.

* **Apple: Leveraging the Freemium Model for App Distribution**

Apple's App Store pioneered the freemium model for app distribution, offering a vast library of apps with a mix of free and paid options. This strategy attracted a large user base, generating revenue from app purchases and in-app advertisements.

* **Airbnb: Transforming the Hospitality Industry with the Sharing Economy**

Airbnb challenged the traditional hotel industry by introducing a peer-to-peer platform that allowed individuals to rent out their homes and apartments. This sharing economy model unlocked new opportunities for homeowners to monetize their properties and provided travelers with unique lodging experiences.

* **Netflix: Pioneering the Subscription Model for Streaming Entertainment**

In the early days of DVDs, Netflix emerged as a revolutionary player in the rental industry, offering a subscription-based service that delivered DVDs to customers' doorsteps. This innovative model disrupted the traditional brick-and-mortar rental model, providing convenience and flexibility to consumers.

* **Uber: Disrupting the Taxi Industry with the On-Demand Model**

Uber revolutionized the taxi industry by introducing a mobile app-based on-demand service that connected riders with drivers. This model eliminated the need for dispatchers and traditional taxi stands, providing riders with greater convenience and flexibility. Uber's success highlights the importance of adapting business models to changing market conditions and consumer preferences. By leveraging technology and embracing the on-demand economy, Uber disrupted the taxi industry and established itself as a global leader in transportation.

> **"Startups don't fail because they lack a product; they fail because they lack customers and a profitable business model"**
>
> **– Steve Blank**

3 – Hidden Revenue Streams

In the pursuit of financial success, income serves as the fuel that propels us towards our objectives.

While traditional notions of income focus solely on monetary gains, a broader perspective reveals a wealth of alternative income streams that can significantly enhance our journey.

Consider your goal as a beacon guiding your income strategies. If your aspiration lies in amassing $1 million, monetary income remains paramount.

However, if your objective is to reach 1 million users, your income metric shifts from money to user engagement.

As you explore alternative income avenues, never lose sight of your ultimate goal. Strive to amplify any factor that accelerates your progress towards that goal.

Key Steps:

1. **Business Model Selection:** Determine the mechanism through which you intend to transform your idea into income. (See: Choosing Your Business Model)
2. **Income Diversification:** Identify non-monetary income generators that align with your business model.
3. **Decision-Makers:** In B2B settings, those who authorize purchases may differ from those who directly pay.

Software developers and marketing managers seeking product adoption exemplify this dynamic.
4. **Engagement Metrics:** User engagement, time spent on the platform, and demonstrated interest can hold significant value. For instance, if your revenue model relies on advertising, a larger active user base translates into more ad impressions and consequently, higher earnings.
5. **Data Monetization:** User data, when ethically collected and utilized, offers substantial value. With user consent, data can be sold to other companies or repurposed into a searchable data warehouse.
6. **Referral Programs:** Encouraging user referrals can lead to an expanded user base and, in turn, increased sales.
7. **Customer Testimonials:** Positive endorsements from key customers enhance product credibility and influence purchasing decisions.
8. **Third-Party Validation:** Favorable product reviews from respected publications can boost sales or user acquisition.
9. **Customer Lifetime Value:** Retaining existing customers is often more cost-effective than acquiring new ones. Explore strategies to maximize revenue from your current customer base.
10. **Process Automation:** If limited resources hinder sales efforts, consider integrating technology to automate processes and increase sales per unit time. For example, a chatbot can streamline customer interactions and boost sales conversions.

Thought-Provoking Questions:

1. What are the unmet needs or pain points of our target audience that we can address through additional income streams?
2. How can we leverage our existing product or service to create new and complementary revenue channels?
3. What are the emerging trends in our industry and how can we capitalize on them to generate new income sources?
4. How can we tap into the expertise and skills of our team members to develop innovative income-generating ideas?
5. What are the potential risks associated with each income stream and how can we mitigate them?
6. How can we test and validate our income-generating ideas before investing significant resources?
7. What are the optimal pricing strategies for our new income streams?
8. What are the hidden assets or resources that we can utilize to create new revenue streams?
9. How can we partner with other businesses to create new income streams?
10. How can we create a marketplace for our product or service?

Income is not merely a financial reward but a potent force that drives your journey towards your desired goals. By embracing alternative income streams, you unlock a world of possibilities and accelerate your path to success.

<u>Inspiring Business Tales:</u>

✷ **The Walt Disney's Merchandising:**
Disney is a prime example of a company that has mastered the art of diversifying its revenue streams. The company's core business is still its theme parks and movies, but it has also generated significant revenue from its merchandising, television networks, and streaming services. This diversification has helped Disney to weather economic downturns and become one of the most valuable brands in the world.

✷ **Shopify's Shipping and Fulfillment:**
Shopify, a popular e-commerce platform, has diversified its revenue streams by offering additional services to its merchants, such as point-of-sale systems, shipping and fulfillment solutions, and capital financing. These add-on services provide Shopify with recurring revenue streams and make it a more comprehensive solution for online businesses.

✷ **Starbucks' Ready-to-eat Meals:**
Starbucks, the global coffeehouse chain, has expanded beyond its core beverage offerings to include a wide range of food items, merchandise, and licensing deals. Their expansion into ready-to-eat meals and snacks has been particularly successful, generating significant revenue growth. Additionally, Starbucks' licensing agreements with grocery stores and other retailers have broadened their reach and brand exposure.

✷ **Skillshare's Business-to-business Solutions:**
Skillshare, an online learning platform, has diversified its revenue streams by introducing business-to-business solutions,

such as Skillshare for Teams, which provides personalized training programs for companies. They have also expanded into offering corporate learning solutions, catering to the needs of large organizations.

✶ **LEGO's Media Powerhouse:**
LEGO, the iconic toymaker, has mastered the art of diversifying its revenue streams. Beyond its core brick sets, LEGO has expanded into a media powerhouse, producing successful movies, video games, and theme parks. Their "LEGO Ideas" platform allows fans to submit their own LEGO set designs, further engaging their audience and generating new product ideas.

> *"Wealth is not about how much money you have. It's about having enough to live the life you want without worrying too much about tomorrow."*
>
> *– Stephen Covey*

4 – The Cost-Cutting Ninja

In the dynamic world of business, cost-cutting & profitability stands as the cornerstone of success.

While revenue growth is often the primary focus, streamlining expenses offers an equally effective path to boosting your bottom line.

By adopting a strategic approach to cost management, you can significantly enhance your financial resilience and pave the way for sustainable growth.

Key Steps:

Step 1: Categorize and Track Expenses
The first step towards expense reduction lies in gaining a comprehensive understanding of your cost structure. Begin by meticulously categorizing all incoming and outgoing expenses. This will provide a clear picture of where your money is being allocated. Regularly monitor these categories to identify trends and potential areas for savings.

Step 2: Dedicate Time for Expense Review
Schedule a designated time each month to scrutinize your expense list. Review each item carefully, questioning its necessity and exploring alternative options. Don't hesitate to challenge assumptions and seek out better deals.

Step 3: Avoid Automated Expenses

Resist the temptation to automate all expenses. Regularly review recurring expenses to ensure they remain aligned with your current needs and budget. Actively approve each expense, fostering a sense of accountability and preventing unnecessary spending.

Step 4: Leverage Market Dynamics

Stay informed about the competitive landscape in your industry. As new players enter the market, they often introduce innovative and cost-effective solutions. Use this to your advantage by negotiating with existing suppliers or exploring new partnerships.

Step 5: Optimize Workforce Utilization

Carefully assess your workforce and identify opportunities to optimize resource allocation. Avoid outsourcing tasks that can be effectively handled by your existing team. This not only saves costs but also preserves institutional knowledge and expertise.

Step 6: Monetize Waste and Surplus

Explore avenues to monetize waste or surplus materials generated during your operations. For instance, consider recycling or selling recyclable materials to generate additional revenue streams.

Step 7: Evaluate Overhead Expenses

Scrutinize overhead expenses such as rent, electricity, and water consumption. Explore potential savings through relocation to a smaller office space, adopting energy-efficient practices, and implementing water conservation measures.

Step 8: Empower Employees for Expense Reduction

Designate an employee to track and manage non-work expenses. Implement an incentive program that rewards them for successfully reducing these expenditures.

Step 9: Modernize Marketing Strategies

Embrace modern marketing methods that offer measurable and predictable returns on investment. Shift away from traditional methods that lack clear performance metrics.

Step 10: Automate Business Processes

Seek opportunities to automate routine tasks and streamline workflows. Explore productivity tools and software solutions that can enhance efficiency and reduce labor costs.

Thought-Provoking Questions:

1. How can you effectively reduce each expense item without compromising business performance or customer satisfaction?
2. Do commissions and other incentive structures align with your overall profitability goals?
3. Are you overpaying for services due to personal relationships with vendors or service providers?
4. Are meetings held efficiently or do they result in wasted time and resources?
5. Are you making the most of your time and prioritizing tasks that drive business growth?
6. Are your employees assigned tasks based on their skills and expertise, or are they underutilized?

7. Are you aware of and taking advantage of government support programs or financial incentives?
8. Are you actively investing surplus funds to generate additional revenue streams?
9. Have you embraced digital document management to eliminate unnecessary printing costs?
10. Have you established clear spending limits for company credit cards to prevent unauthorized charges?

By implementing these strategies and addressing the key questions outlined above, you can effectively reduce expenses, boost profitability, and achieve sustainable success in your business endeavors.

Inspiring Business Tales:

✴ **Aldi's Discount Supermarket Efficiency**
Aldi, the discount supermarket chain, has a business model focused on extreme cost-cutting measures to offer low prices. These include a limited product selection, simple store layouts, and a focus on private-label brands. Aldi's approach has not only allowed it to compete with larger supermarket chains but also to expand rapidly in various international markets.

✴ **Southwest Airlines and Fuel Hedging**
In the early 2000s, Southwest Airlines gained a competitive advantage through successful fuel hedging, which protected the airline against rising fuel costs. This strategy allowed Southwest to maintain lower operational costs compared to competitors, contributing to its profitability and growth in the airline industry.

* **Amazon Web Services (AWS)**
AWS grew out of Amazon's own need for scalable, efficient cloud computing infrastructure. By offering its excess server capacity to other businesses, Amazon turned a cost center into a profitable and dominant cloud services provider.

* **Uber's Use of Independent Contractors**
Uber's business model relies on independent contractors as drivers rather than full-time employees. This strategy significantly cuts costs related to wages, benefits, and vehicle maintenance. By avoiding the overhead costs typical of traditional taxi services, Uber has been able to expand quickly and offer competitive pricing.

* **YouTube's User-Generated Content Model**
YouTube's platform is primarily based on user-generated content, significantly cutting costs associated with content creation. This model allows YouTube to host a vast amount of content without the large investment typically required for production, contributing to its status as the leading video-sharing platform.

> *"The real cost of a four-dollar-a-day coffee habit over 20 years is $51,833.79. That's the power of the Compound Effect."*
>
> *— Darren Hardy*

5 – How to Set Key Performance Indicators

Just as a car's dashboard provides crucial information about its performance, establishing key performance indicators (KPIs) is essential for navigating your business towards success.

Before starting on your entrepreneurial journey, it's crucial to define the metrics that will guide your path and measure your progress.

Imagine you're stepping into your car, ready to start your day. As you turn the ignition, the dashboard lights up, displaying various indicators: speed, RPM, fuel level, engine temperature, and oil pressure.

While we often disregard these indicators, they play a critical role in ensuring a smooth and efficient journey.

Similarly, in the realm of business, KPIs serve as the compass that guides you towards your desired destination. They provide a clear and objective assessment of your company's performance, enabling you to make informed decisions and course-correct when necessary.

Key Steps:

1. **Quantify Your Goal:** Set specific, measurable, and achievable goals for your business. Don't just wish for

success; translate your aspirations into tangible targets. For instance, instead of aiming to make "a lot of money," set a goal of achieving "$1 million in net profit within the next year" or "acquiring 3 million new customers by December."

2. **Break Down Your Goal:** Divide your overall goal into smaller, manageable milestones. To achieve the $1 million net profit target, you'll need to generate an average monthly revenue of $80,000 to $85,000. Considering you're starting from zero, factor in a gradual revenue increase.

3. **Set Monthly Targets:** Determine achievable monthly targets that align with your overall goal. For example, aim to reach $20,000 in revenue during the first month.

4. **Calculate Your Monthly Increase Rate:** To achieve the $1 million goal, you'll need an average monthly increase rate of 25%. This means surpassing your previous month's results by 25% each month.

5. **Identify Performance Drivers:** Analyze the factors that contribute to your revenue growth. If your goal is to achieve a 25% monthly increase, determine how many sales, expenses, and promotions are required to achieve this growth.

6. **Determine Sales Conversion Rate:** Calculate your average sales conversion rate, which is the percentage of people who make a purchase after exposure to your promotional efforts. For instance, if you convert 2% of your promotional reach into sales, then you need to promote to 10,000 people to achieve your first-month sales target.

7. **Establish Advertising Performance:** Calculate your advertising ROI (return on investment), which measures the effectiveness of your promotional spending. If you

spend $1,000 to promote to 1,000 people and generate $2,000 in sales, your advertising ROI is 200%.
8. **Identify Critical KPIs:** Summarize your key performance indicators: monthly turnover targets, monthly increase rate, sales conversion rate, and advertising performance.
9. **Continuous Monitoring:** Regularly monitor these KPIs to assess your progress and identify areas for improvement. If a KPI deviates from your target, analyze the underlying factors and make adjustments accordingly.
10. **Prioritize Tasks:** Based on your KPI analysis, prioritize tasks that contribute directly to achieving your goals. Focus your efforts on the activities that move the needle and drive business growth.

Thought-Provoking Questions:

1. **Reality Check:** Are Your KPIs Realistic? Examine the numbers you encounter when determining indicators. Are they grounded in reality or merely wishful thinking? Setting unrealistic targets, such as a 200% increase in AD ROI when the current rate is 20%, can lead to disappointment and hinder progress.
2. **Scenario Planning:** Prepare for Unforeseen Challenges. Anticipate potential roadblocks and establish clear action plans accordingly. Define "good," "bad," and "medium" scenarios for each goal, outlining the decisions you'll make at each stage. This proactive approach ensures you're well-equipped to adapt to changing circumstances.

3. **Shared Responsibility:** Enlist Employee Engagement. Don't isolate yourself in the pursuit of your goals. Share your targets with your employees and motivate them to contribute to their respective KPI areas. This collaborative approach fosters a sense of ownership and drives collective performance improvement.
4. **Sustaining Momentum:** Assess Resource Availability. Assess your capacity to maintain the intensity required to achieve your KPI targets. Evaluate your energy levels, financial resources, and overall motivation to ensure you can sustain the necessary drive throughout the journey.
5. **KPI Overload:** Avoid information overload by streamlining your KPI selection. Prioritize the most critical indicators, keeping your daily review time within a manageable 15 seconds. Delegate less critical KPIs to relevant team members, ensuring everyone is focused on the most impactful metrics.
6. **Empowering Employees:** Recognize that every employee, regardless of their perceived role, can contribute to achieving your goals. Engage seemingly irrelevant employees by assigning them relevant KPIs that measure their ability to perform at their best. Encourage them to propose their own KPIs, fostering a sense of ownership and engagement.
7. **Listen:** What are your employees telling you? What are your employees telling you about their work, their customers, and the overall state of the business? Your employees are on the front lines, so their insights can be invaluable.
8. **Trends:** What are your industry trends? What are the latest trends in your industry, and how are they impacting your business? You need to be aware of

industry trends so that you can identify KPIs that will help you stay ahead of the curve.
9. **Goals:** What are your goals for your KPIs? What do you want to achieve by tracking these KPIs? Do you want to improve efficiency, increase sales, or reduce costs? Once you know your goals, you can start to develop a plan for tracking and using your KPIs effectively.
10. **Priority:** What are the most important goals and objectives of your business? What do you want to achieve in the next year, five years, or ten years? Once you know your goals, you can start to identify the KPIs that will measure your progress towards them.

Establishing and tracking KPIs is not just a bureaucratic exercise; it's the foundation of a successful business.

Understanding and managing key indicators allows you to transform your company from a haphazard operation into a well-oiled machine, moving in unison towards your target destination. This success hinges on setting realistic and measurable goals, breaking them down into manageable milestones, and continuously tracking your progress.

With KPIs as your guide, you'll navigate the entrepreneurial landscape with confidence and achieve sustainable success.

Inspiring Business Tales:

* **Airbnb's Occupancy and User Experience KPIs**

Airbnb measures KPIs like occupancy rates, average daily rates, and guest satisfaction to gauge its performance in the hospitality industry. These KPIs help Airbnb understand market trends, host performance, and areas where the user experience can be improved.

✷ **Domino's Pizza Turnaround & Delivery Efficiency**
Domino's focuses on KPIs related to delivery time and order accuracy, crucial for customer satisfaction in the fast-food industry. By improving these metrics, Domino's turned its business around, reinforcing its position as a leading pizza delivery company.

✷ **Netflix and Viewer Engagement Metrics**
Netflix's success in content creation is partly due to its focus on detailed viewer engagement metrics, such as watch time, completion rates, and search patterns. These KPIs inform Netflix's decisions on what type of content to produce or acquire, leading to highly successful original series and a robust content library tailored to viewer preferences.

✷ **Zara's Inventory Turnover**
Zara, the fast-fashion retailer, tracks inventory turnover as a critical KPI to maintain its rapid production cycle and minimize overstock. This focus enables Zara to quickly respond to fashion trends, reduce waste, and ensure that its stores are always stocked with fresh and desirable apparel.

> *"If you can't measure it,*
> *you can't improve it"*
> *—Peter Drucker*

6 – Build Profitable Pricing Models

Consumer behavior often takes a different turn when financial decisions are involved. You have to be ready for that.

To effectively entice customers to purchase your product or service, it is crucial to provide them with a compelling range of options.

The initial stage of the ideation process should focus on identifying problems or unmet needs from the customer's perspective. Prioritizing the "problem" is essential, as without a problem to solve, there is no product or service to sell.

Once a genuine customer need has been identified, the focus shifts to generating ideas that effectively address that need. It is crucial to validate the existence and importance of the problem before investing time and resources into developing solutions.

Two critical questions need to be answered before proceeding with product development:

1. Are customers willing to pay to solve this problem?
2. If so, what is the maximum amount they are willing to pay for a solution?

Without addressing these questions, the product or service risks failing from the outset. If customers are accustomed to living with the problem or believe it is insignificant enough to warrant no financial investment, no matter how effectively the problem is solved, the venture is likely to be unsuccessful.

Key Steps:

1. **Clearly Define the Solution:** Articulate the value proposition of your product or service.
2. **Determine the Business Model:** Identify the revenue streams that support your business.
3. **Explore Non-Monetary Valuables:** Consider alternative forms of value exchange beyond monetary transactions.
4. **Analyze Competitor Pricing:** Research and understand the pricing strategies of similar products or services.
5. **Evaluate Cost Structure:** Carefully assess the costs associated with your product or service.
6. **Establish Profit Margin:** Calculate the profit margin you aim to achieve.
7. **Balance Profitability and Market Positioning:** Consider offering discounted prices to increase market share while maintaining profitability
8. **Product Differentiation and Pricing:** Set prices based on the competitive advantage and unique value proposition of your product or service
9. **Dynamic Pricing for Fluctuating Demand:** Employ dynamic pricing strategies to adjust prices based on variations in demand (e.g., flight tickets, hotel rates)
10. **Continuous Price Optimization:** Regularly evaluate and refine pricing strategies based on market feedback and performance data

Thought-Provoking Questions:

1. **Price Paradox:** Despite high sales volumes, profits remain elusive. What could be the reason? You might be overlooking hidden expenses associated with each sale. For instance, if customer service demands surge due to increased sales, overtime costs could erode your profit margins. Similarly, higher return rates from price-sensitive customers could inflate shipping expenses.
2. **Discount Dependence:** Why does my business rely on constant discounting to attract customers? Discounts, when used excessively, lose their effectiveness. Savvy customers anticipate discounts and defer purchases until promotional periods. To break this cycle, consider offering value-added services or creating a sense of urgency through limited-time promotions.
3. **Competitor Conundrum:** My rival's prices are inexplicably lower, how is that possible? Your competitor might be employing the "pull to shop" strategy. They may knowingly incur losses on certain products to attract customers to their store, where they can generate substantial profits from other items.
4. **Pricing in a Monopoly:** How do I determine prices without direct competitors? While the simplest approach is to follow cost-plus pricing, a more strategic approach is to consider the purchasing power of your target customer base. If their purchasing power is high, consider lowering prices to levels you might not otherwise consider.
5. **Caught in a Pricing Squeeze:** Neither high nor low prices yield sales. What can I do? Profitability in the FMCG sector often hinges on economies of scale. For

instance, buying peaches in bulk significantly reduces the unit cost compared to purchasing individual kilograms. This allows you to lower your selling price while maintaining profitability.
6. **Bulk Buying Dilemma:** How do I balance bulk purchases with product perishability? The key lies in efficient inventory management and demand forecasting. By accurately predicting sales and optimizing order quantities, you can minimize spoilage and maximize the benefits of bulk buying.
7. **Perceived Value vs. Actual Cost:** How do I reconcile the discrepancy between the perceived value of my product or service and its actual cost? Bridging this gap requires effective marketing and communication strategies. Emphasize the unique value proposition of your offering, highlighting how it addresses customer needs and surpasses their expectations. This can help justify pricing that reflects the true value of your product or service.
8. **Pricing for Different Customer Segments:** How do I tailor my pricing strategy to cater to different customer segments with varying price sensitivities? Segmenting your customer base based on demographics, purchase behavior, and willingness to pay allows you to implement targeted pricing strategies. For price-sensitive segments, consider offering value-based pricing or tiered pricing models. For segments with higher purchasing power, consider premium pricing or premium features.
9. **Pricing for New vs. Established Products:** How do I determine the appropriate pricing strategy for new products versus established ones? New products often require introductory pricing to gain market share and

establish a customer base. Once a product is established and has a loyal customer following, a higher profit margin can be pursued. However, it's crucial to maintain a balance between profitability and customer satisfaction.
10. **Pricing for Global Expansion:** How do I adapt my pricing strategy when expanding into international markets? Consider factors such as local purchasing power, competitive landscape, and cultural preferences when setting prices for international markets. Conduct thorough market research to understand the pricing expectations and sensitivities of consumers in each region.

Effective pricing is an ongoing process that requires continuous evaluation and adaptation. By understanding customer behavior, addressing genuine needs, and implementing strategic pricing strategies, businesses can position themselves for long-term success.

Inspiring Business Tales:

✴ **J.Crew's High-Low Pricing Strategy**
J.Crew implemented a high-low pricing strategy, mixing high-end items with more affordable pieces. This approach aimed to attract a broader customer base - from budget shoppers to those seeking premium products. This strategy helped J.Crew to position itself uniquely in the retail clothing market, appealing to a diverse range of consumers.

✴ **Starbucks and the Psychology of Cup Sizes**

Starbucks cleverly designed its cup sizes - Tall, Grande, Venti, and Trenta - to create a perception of value. The price difference between sizes is relatively small, encouraging customers to opt for a larger size. This upselling strategy, known as "price anchoring," subtly encourages customers to spend more than they initially might have planned, increasing the average transaction size.

* **Dynamic Pricing of Uber**

Uber employs a dynamic pricing model, known as "surge pricing," where fares increase during times of high demand. This pricing strategy helps balance supply and demand, incentivizes drivers to be available during busy times, and allows Uber to maximize revenue during peak periods.

* **Apple's Skimming Price Strategy**

Apple often employs a price skimming strategy, launching products at a high price point and gradually lowering prices over time. This approach allows Apple to maximize profits from early adopters who are willing to pay a premium and later capture the more price-sensitive segment of the market.

* **The Economist Decoy Pricing in Subscriptions**

The Economist once offered three subscription options: online-only for $59, print-only for $125, and print-and-web for $125. The print-only option served as a decoy, making the combined option seem more valuable. This decoy pricing strategy effectively encouraged subscribers to choose the more expensive combined option, perceiving it as a better deal.

* **Price Discrimination in Airlines**

Airlines use price discrimination, charging different prices for the same seat based on factors like booking time, route demand, and customer segment. This strategy allows airlines to maximize revenue by capturing a higher willingness to pay from certain customer segments while filling up remaining seats at lower prices.

> **"You know you're priced right when your customers complain but buy anyway."**
>
> **— *John Harrison***

7 – Words that Sell: The Power of Persuasive Copywriting

In the competitive world of digital products, capturing a customer's attention from the very first encounter is crucial.

The initial impression can make or break a purchase decision, and often, this decision is made within mere seconds.

While factors like reliability and price play a role in the final decision, the first impression sets the tone and influences the customer's perception of the product.

The visual appeal of a product is a significant factor in shaping that first impression. A product's design and aesthetics can evoke emotions, convey its purpose, and differentiate it from competitors.

A well-designed product speaks volumes about the brand's attention to detail, innovation, and commitment to providing a positive user experience.

The product phrase that introduces a product serves as the brand's first introduction to potential customers. It's the verbal equivalent of a product's design, and it should be crafted with the same level of care and attention.

Key Steps:

1. Establish Differentiation: Clearly articulate what sets the product apart from competitors and why it's worth considering.
2. Address Customer Pain Points: Acknowledge and address the problem or pain point that the product aims to solve.
3. Be Concise and Clear: Convey the product's essence and value proposition in a simple, jargon-free manner.
4. Signal Positive Change: Highlight how the product will positively impact the customer's life.
5. Speak in Customer Language: Use language that resonates with the target audience and aligns with their understanding.
6. Address Unanswered Questions: Anticipate and address the customer's key questions or concerns.
7. Emphasize Problem-Solving: Focus on the problem and its solution, rather than listing product features.
8. Tailor Messaging: Adapt the product phrase to suit different customer personas and communication channels.
9. Resonate: Product phrase should resonate with your customer's innermost feelings, evoking a sense of empathy and recognition of their pain point. Make them feel heard and validated in their search for a solution.
10. Treasure: Product phrase should unveil a hidden treasure, revealing the existence of a solution that has long been sought by your customer.

In the digital world, a product or service's success often hinges on its landing page. This dedicated webpage acts as the first impression, the crucial point where visitors convert into leads or customers. It's here that clear, compelling copy plays a vital role.

Like a newborn needing the right environment to thrive, your product requires effective landing page copy to flourish.

This entails crafting benefit-driven headlines, engaging body text, and powerful calls to action. By addressing your audience's desires and offering solutions, you guide them towards conversion.

First impressions matter. Invest in high-quality landing page copy from the very beginning. It's not just a launchpad for your product; it's the foundation of its digital success story.

A high-converting landing page isn't just about a pretty design; it also needs persuasive and strategically placed marketing copy to drive conversions. Here are the essential elements:

1. **Headline:**
   - Clear and concise: Grab attention and communicate your value proposition instantly.
   - Compelling: Speak directly to your audience's pain points and desires.
   - Benefit-driven: Highlight the benefits of taking the desired action.

2. **Subheadings:**
   - Break up your copy and enhance readability.

- Add further detail and explanation to your main headline.
- Use strong calls to action (CTAs) to encourage conversion.

3. **Body copy:**
   - Benefit-focused: Explain how your product or service solves your target audience's problems.
   - Action-oriented: Use strong verbs and clear instructions to guide visitors towards conversion.
   - Storytelling: Engage your audience and build trust through compelling stories.
   - Credible and authentic: Use clear, concise language and avoid jargon.
   - Personalized: Address your audience directly and speak to their specific needs and desires.

4. **Call to action (CTA):**
   - Clear and concise: Tell visitors what you want them to do next.
   - Benefit-driven: Reiterate the value proposition of taking action.
   - High contrast and visually appealing: Make the CTA button stand out.
   - Multiple CTAs throughout the page: Increase conversion opportunities.

5. **Social proof:**
   - Testimonials: Showcase positive feedback from satisfied customers.
   - Case studies: Demonstrate the success of your product or service with real examples.

- Logos and awards: Build trust and credibility by displaying industry recognition.
- Numbers and statistics: Quantify the benefits of your offer.

6. **Additional elements:**
   - Images and videos: Visually engage your audience and tell your story.
   - Bullet points and numbered lists: Make your copy easier to read and understand.
   - Guarantee or warranty: Reduce risk and increase trust.
   - Contact information: Make it easy for visitors to get in touch.
   - Mobile-friendly design: Ensure your landing page looks great and functions seamlessly on all devices.

Remember:
- Test and iterate: Continuously test different versions of your landing page copy and optimize for maximum conversions.
- Use A/B testing: Compare two versions of your landing page to see which one performs better.
- Track your results: Monitor your conversion rate and other key metrics to measure the effectiveness of your landing page copy.

By incorporating these essential elements and best practices, you can create high-converting landing page copy that drives results and fuels your business growth.

Thought-Provoking Questions:

1. If my product were a person, what would their personality be like? What kind of language would they use to describe themselves and the problems they solve?
2. What is the hidden fear or insecurity that my product can address? How can I use the product phrase to tap into this emotional undercurrent and offer a sense of relief or empowerment?
3. What is the unspoken desire or aspiration that my product can help fulfill? How can I frame the product phrase in a way that resonates with this deeper longing and sparks a sense of excitement and possibility?
4. What kind of community or tribe does my product belong to? What shared values, beliefs, or passions do these people have? How can I use the product phrase to connect with this community and establish a sense of belonging?
5. What is the most common misconception or myth about my product category? Can I use the product phrase to challenge this misconception and introduce a fresh perspective that captures the customer's attention?
6. What is the most effective way to shock or surprise my customer with my product phrase? Can I create a moment of unexpected delight or intrigue that leaves a lasting impression?
7. What is the most powerful way to leverage storytelling in my product phrase? Can I weave a compelling narrative that showcases the transformative impact of my product in real-world scenarios?
8. What is the most effective way to incorporate humor or wit into my product phrase? Can I create a sense of

lightheartedness and relatability that breaks down barriers and engages the customer on a personal level?
9. What is the most memorable way to use sensory language to describe my product? Can I evoke vivid imagery and emotional experiences that connect with the customer's senses and leave a lasting imprint?
10. What is the most effective way to use social proof or testimonials to reinforce the value proposition of my product phrase? Can I incorporate authentic voices from satisfied customers to build trust and credibility?

Inspiring Business Tales:

Airbnb's "*Live There, Don't Just Visit*":
This campaign focused on the experience of living like a local in a new city rather than simply staying in a hotel room. The body copy then details authentic local experiences, making travelers feel like part of the community.

Apple's "Think Different" campaign:
This campaign celebrated nonconformity and creativity, appealing to Apple's target audience of innovators and independent thinkers. The campaign's powerful and inspiring message helped Apple build a loyal following and become one of the most valuable companies in the world.

Dropbox's "*Never lose a file again*":
This body copy speaks directly to a common pain point for users, offering a simple and effective solution that provides peace of mind.

Grammarly's "*Write confidently. Write clearly. Write like a pro*":
This body copy addresses multiple pain points, offering a comprehensive solution for improved writing skills and confidence.

Asana's "*Get organized. Get things done*":
This concise subheading captures the essence of Asana's value proposition: increased productivity through organization. The body copy provides concrete examples of how Asana helps teams manage tasks, collaborate effectively, and achieve their goals.

Bumble's "*Make the first move. It's your turn*":
This subheading empowers women by challenging traditional dating norms. The body copy emphasizes Bumble's female-first approach, creating a safe and inclusive environment for women to initiate connections.

Uber Eats:
- Subheading: "*Hangry? We got you.*"
- Body copy: "*Skip the kitchen, skip the crowds, and get your favorite food delivered straight to your door. Because life's too short for cooking*"

Slack:
- Subheading: "*Get stuff done. Together.*"
- Body copy: "*Tired of endless email chains and confusing communication? Slack brings your team together in one place, making collaboration and productivity a breeze. Plus, it's fun to use!*"

Headspace:

- Subheading: *"Take 10 minutes to find your calm."*
- Body copy: *"Take a break from the daily grind and find your inner peace with Headspace. Guided meditations, sleep stories, and mindfulness exercises help you manage stress, improve focus, and sleep better."*

Tesla:

- Subheading: *"Drive the future. Electric. Sustainable. Tesla."*
- Body copy: *"Join the electric revolution with Tesla. Our cutting-edge vehicles combine performance and sustainability, offering an exhilarating driving experience while contributing to a greener planet."*

TED Talks:

- Subheading: *"Ideas Worth Spreading. Minds Worth Opening."*
- Body copy: *"TED Talks bring the world's most inspiring ideas to your fingertips. Explore diverse topics, challenge your perspectives, and join a global community passionate about change."*

Starbucks:

- Subheading: *"Sip, Savor, Connect."*
- Body copy: *"Starbucks is more than coffee; it's a moment of connection. Enjoy handcrafted beverages in a welcoming atmosphere, where every cup tells a story of quality and community."*

Fitbit:

- Subheading: *"Track Your Progress. Ignite Your Potential."*

- Body copy: "*Fitbit is your fitness companion, monitoring every step, heartbeat, and achievement. Elevate your wellness journey and unlock the best version of yourself.*"

National Geographic:
- Subheading: "*Explore. Understand. Protect.*"
- Body copy: "*National Geographic takes you on a journey of discovery. With breathtaking visuals and compelling storytelling, we inspire a deeper understanding of our planet and its wonders.*"

Spotify:
- Subheading: "*Your Soundtrack to Life. Anywhere, Anytime.*"
- Body copy: "*Spotify curates the perfect soundtrack for your moments. With a vast library, personalized playlists, and seamless listening, immerse yourself in the joy of music.*"

Etsy:
- Subheading: "*Handmade, Vintage, Unique Finds.*"
- Body copy: "*Etsy is a marketplace of creativity. Explore one-of-a-kind treasures crafted by independent sellers worldwide, turning every purchase into a meaningful story.*"

> **"Nobody reads ads. People read what interests them. Sometimes it's an ad."**
>
> **- Howard Gossage**

8 – Validate Your Product Idea Before You Build It

Imagine a world where you could predict the success of your product idea with certainty, before investing a dime in development.

Sounds like a dream, right? Well, wake up! This dream can be your reality with market simulation.

Developing a product is expensive. Time, money, and effort are poured into bringing your vision to life. But what if, after all that hard work, your product flops?

To avoid this painful scenario, testing your idea before development is crucial.

Market simulation allows you to experiment with different options for your product, such as:

- **Price points:** Discover the optimal price that maximizes revenue, not just profit.
- **Marketing language:** Craft compelling messaging that resonates with your target audience.
- **Solutions:** Validate that your product solves a genuine problem and fulfills a need.

By testing these variables, you can gain valuable insights and make informed decisions about your product before you even write a single line of code.

Price is a powerful tool that can impact everything from customer perception to profitability. Market simulation allows you to explore different price points and see how they affect key metrics like:

- Conversion rate: The percentage of visitors who actually buy your product.
- Return rate: The percentage of customers who return your product.
- Customer lifetime value (CLV): The total revenue a customer generates over their lifetime.

By understanding the relationship between price and these metrics, you can identify the "sweet spot" that maximizes your profit and customer satisfaction.

Testing Methods for Every Budget

The good news is that market simulation doesn't require a hefty budget. Here are a few effective methods you can use:

- **Welcome Page:** Create a simple website showcasing your product features and a "buy" button. Capture leads by requesting email addresses or phone numbers. If you see a 10% conversion rate or higher, your idea has potential.
- **One-on-One Meetings:** Prepare variations of your product and questions for potential customers. Observe their reactions and choices to gain valuable insights.
- **Surveys:** Craft a survey using Google Forms and distribute it to individuals who fit your target audience.

Analyze their responses to identify strengths and weaknesses of your concept.
- **Community Support:** Launch a crowdfunding campaign on sites like Kickstarter or Indiegogo. Not only will you raise funds, but you'll also gauge the community's interest in your product.
- **Manpower:** Mimic the product experience without actual development. Perform tasks manually that would be automated in the final product.
- **Prototype:** Develop a basic version of your product with core features. If it generates interest despite its simplicity, you can confidently invest in further development.

Key Steps:

1. Define your target audience: Who are you trying to reach with your product? What are their needs and pain points?
2. Choose your testing method: Will you use a welcome page, one-on-one meetings, surveys, community support, manpower, or a prototype?
3. Develop your variations: Create different versions of your product with varying price points, marketing language, or solutions.
4. Prepare your test materials: This could include a website, presentation, or survey questions.
5. Recruit participants: Find people who fit your target audience to test your variations.
6. Run your test: Present your variations to participants and collect their feedback.
7. Analyze your data: Look for trends and patterns in the data to identify which variations perform best.

8. Draw conclusions: Based on your findings, decide which version of your product has the most potential.
9. Iterate and refine: Based on your learnings, make changes to your product and test again.
10. Launch your product: Once you're confident in your product, launch it to the market.

Thought-Provoking Questions:

1. Are we testing the right problem? Is our focus on the core issue our target audience truly faces, or are we addressing a symptom of a larger problem?
2. Are we framing our solution accurately? Does our marketing message clearly articulate how our product solves the problem in a way that resonates with the target audience's language and understanding?
3. Are we testing the right pricing model? Are we exploring a sufficient range of price points and considering different pricing strategies (e.g., subscription, freemium) to determine the optimal value proposition?
4. Are we simulating a realistic customer journey? Does our simulation realistically replicate the touchpoints and interactions a customer would encounter when discovering, evaluating, and purchasing our product?
5. Are we relying on the right metrics? Are we focusing on the most relevant metrics that accurately reflect customer behavior and predict long-term success (e.g., lifetime value, churn rate), or are we prioritizing vanity metrics like website traffic? Utilize statistical significance tools to ensure the reliability of your market simulation results

6. Are we including potential objections and negative scenarios? Does our simulation account for potential customer concerns, doubts, and negative feedback, allowing us to identify and address them proactively?
7. Are we considering alternative solutions and competitors? Are we testing our product against existing solutions and understanding how our value proposition differentiates us in the market?
8. Are we integrating feedback and iterating quickly? Are we actively collecting and analyzing feedback from participants to refine our product and marketing message throughout the simulation process?
9. Are we testing for cultural and demographic biases? Are we ensuring our simulation reaches a diverse audience and that our findings are not skewed by unconscious biases?
10. Are we measuring the right emotions? Are we capturing the emotional responses of participants (e.g., excitement, frustration, satisfaction) to gain deeper insights into their overall experience with our product?

You can increase your chances of developing a successful product that meets the needs of your target audience by following these steps.

Market simulation is not about absolute certainty. It's about reducing risk and making informed decisions. By testing your ideas early and often, you can increase your chances of building a product that people love and that thrives in the market.

Don't let your dream product become a costly mistake. Start simulating your market today!

Inspiring Business Tales:

Dropbox:
Dropbox famously used a single landing page with a clear and concise value proposition to drive early user adoption. They focused on collecting email addresses, and once they had a critical mass, they launched their product to much fanfare. This simple but effective marketing simulation strategy allowed them to validate their idea and build a loyal user base before investing heavily in development.

Airbnb:
Airbnb initially struggled to gain traction, but they turned things around by focusing on marketing simulation. They created a mock website and used it to test different concepts and messaging with potential customers. This helped them refine their value proposition and attract early adopters, ultimately leading them to become a dominant force in the travel industry.

Spotify:
Spotify uses a combination of machine learning and human curation to personalize its music recommendations. They constantly test and refine their algorithms to ensure they are delivering the best possible listening experience for their users. This focus on data and personalization has helped them become one of the most popular music streaming services in the world.

Pepsi's Pepsi Challenge:
Pepsi's famous blind taste test, the Pepsi Challenge, was a marketing campaign that showed the power of consumer

preferences. It highlighted the importance of understanding and catering to consumer tastes.

Unilever:
Unilever, a global consumer goods company, uses AI-powered marketing simulation to predict the effectiveness of their advertising campaigns. They analyze data on consumer behavior and media consumption to create targeted campaigns that are more likely to resonate with their audience.

Samsung:
Samsung uses simulation software to test the durability and performance of their smartphones and other electronic devices. This helps them identify potential issues and improve the quality of their products before launch.

Domino's Pizza:
Domino's uses data analytics to predict customer demand and optimize their delivery routes. This simulation helps them ensure efficient delivery and timely service, improving customer satisfaction.

> *"Testing leads to failure, and failure leads to understanding."*
>
> *— Burt Rutan*

9 – Pivot from Stagnation to Success

Is your business hitting a wall, unable to achieve its full potential? You may be facing a broken business model, undermined by a dynamic landscape of shifting variables.

Don't despair. By actively seeking out improvements, you can revitalize your business and achieve renewed growth.

Success depends on a complex interplay of numerous variable factors, and just like any system, these variables can become unbalanced over time, leading to dysfunction.

This can manifest as a decline in revenue, even without any apparent changes in your operations. Identifying the root cause of this decline requires thorough introspection and an open mind.

Key Steps:

1. **Unearth your Unfair Advantage:** Differentiate your business from the competition by identifying your "unfair advantage" - a unique selling proposition that sets you apart.
2. **Simplify, Simplify, Simplify:** Complexity breeds inefficiency. Streamline your operations and offerings for maximum effectiveness.
3. **Niche Down:** Instead of chasing broad appeal, focus on serving a specific, well-defined customer segment. This

allows you to tailor your offerings and messaging for maximum impact.
4. **Business Model Innovation:** Explore alternative ways to deliver your value proposition. Consider new revenue streams, subscriptions, partnerships, or distribution channels.
5. **Customer & Price Differentiation:** Offer tiered pricing based on customer demographics or feature sets. This can maximize revenue while attracting diverse customer segments.
6. **Rethink your Marketing:** Conduct a thorough analysis of your marketing channels. Identify areas for improvement and explore new markets, new countries, new channels, that may be more effective.
7. **Listen to your Customers:** Engage with customers who have fallen away and understand their reasons for doing so. Their feedback can provide valuable insights for improvement. Refine your messaging. Rethink how you communicate your value proposition to resonate better with your target audience.
8. **Embrace Technology:** Stay informed about emerging technologies and assess their potential to revolutionize your business model.
9. **Seek Investment:** If capital is a constraint, consider seeking external funding to accelerate growth and overcome financial hurdles.
10. **Internal Audit:** Reflect on employee satisfaction within your organization. Happy employees are essential for delivering a positive customer experience.

Thought-Provoking Questions:

1. **Problem Evolution:** Has the problem your business addresses become less relevant? Is the need you fulfill waning?
2. **Emerging Competitors:** Are there new players in the market that you're unaware of? Are they posing a threat to your market share?
3. **Comparative Analysis:** Are you keeping pace with the competition? Benchmark your progress against your competitors to identify areas for improvement.
4. **Self-Assessment:** Are you passionate about your business? Are you fully committed to its success? This can significantly impact your decision-making and drive.
5. **Experimentation:** Are you trying different approaches to overcome crucial challenges? Continuous experimentation and analysis are key to optimizing your business model.
6. **Economic and Emotional Factors:** Consider external factors that might be impacting your customers. Is there a looming economic crisis or a change in consumer sentiment?
7. **Speed:** Are you a marathoner among the sprinters? You think you have improved a lot compared to last year, but if your competitors are outpacing you, you might be slow.
8. **Check Assumptions:** Are your assumptions about your market still valid? Regularly reassess your target audience and market conditions to ensure your understanding remains accurate.
9. **Bug:** Could there be a major technical issue with your product that you didn't realise? Set up alert structures to

ensure that sign up, paywall or other critical features are working properly.
10. **Move On:** Could it be time to admit defeat and move on to another business idea with greater potential?

Inspiring Business Tales:

* **Burbn to Instagram:**
Originally called Burbn, it aimed to be a location-based check-in app like Foursquare. But with limited user adoption, the founders pivoted to focus on mobile photo sharing, adding filters and a strong social element. This transformed Instagram into the global phenomenon it is today.

* **Justin.tv to Twitch:**
Founded as Justin.tv, it primarily focused on live streaming of unscripted events. However, the platform found its niche in gaming live streams. They pivoted to focus on esports and video game streaming, becoming the go-to platform for gamers and viewers worldwide.

* **Musical.ly to TikTok:**
Originally called Musical.ly, it focused on short-form music videos. Recognizing the potential for broader content, they pivoted to allow users to create and share videos across various categories. This move propelled TikTok to become a global phenomenon, especially among young audiences.

* **GoPro**
Founded as a website for surfers to share photos and videos, GoPro realized the potential for capturing action-packed footage. They pivoted to develop a small, durable camera

specifically designed for capturing extreme sports and adventure experiences. This innovative approach made GoPro a household name and redefined action photography.

* **Twitter: From Odeo to Social Networking**
Twitter began as Odeo, a platform for finding and subscribing to podcasts. When Apple's iTunes began dominating the podcast market, Odeo's founders, including Jack Dorsey, pivoted to a new idea - a microblogging platform that eventually became Twitter.

* **Starbucks: From Selling Beans to Brewing Coffee**
Starbucks initially sold high-quality coffee beans and equipment for brewing coffee at home. Howard Schultz, after a trip to Italy, was inspired to transform Starbucks into a café that served brewed coffee and espresso drinks.

* **Nintendo: From Playing Cards to Video Games**
Nintendo began as a company producing handmade playing cards. After several unsuccessful attempts in different businesses, including a taxi service and love hotels, Nintendo found success in the video game industry.

* **PayPal: From Encryption Software to Payments**
PayPal started as Confinity, a company developing security software for handheld devices. Realizing the potential of a digital wallet, the company shifted focus to building a simple and secure platform for online payments.

* **YouTube: From a Dating Site to Video Sharing**
YouTube initially started as a video dating site named "Tune In Hook Up". The founders shifted to a general video sharing platform after the original concept didn't take off.

* **Nokia: From Paper Mills to Telecommunications**
Nokia started as a paper mill operation in Finland. Over the years, Nokia pivoted through various industries, including rubber and cable, before finding massive success in telecommunications. At its peak, Nokia was the world's largest mobile phone manufacturer, but when the smartphone era started, it could not pivot again.

* **BlackBerry's Resistance to Smartphone Trends**
BlackBerry, known for its business-oriented smartphones with physical keyboards, failed to pivot when consumer preferences shifted towards touchscreens and app-centric devices, as popularized by the iPhone and Android smartphones. BlackBerry's reluctance to adapt its hardware and software led to a drastic loss in market share and relevance in the smartphone market.

* **Kodak's Delay in Embracing Digital Photography**
Kodak, a dominant player in the photographic film industry, was slow to pivot to digital photography, despite inventing the first digital camera. Kodak's hesitation to fully embrace digital, fearing it would cannibalize its film business, led to a significant decline in market share and eventual bankruptcy in 2012.

> *"Do not judge me by my success. Judge me by how many times I fell down and got back up again."*
>
> — **Nelson Mandela**

Developing a Product That Users Will Fall in Love With

New to building a digital product? In this section, we will discuss the process of turning a business idea into a reality.

We will cover how to find the team members who will bring your idea to life, what to keep in mind when designing, and more.

The most important thing is for your idea to be perceived, understood, and appreciated in the way you expect it to be when it meets users. To achieve this, there are many steps we need to take.

1 – Build & Manage a Winning Team

Building a strong team is the cornerstone of any successful startup. How to win all those talented people?

It's not just about finding the right people; it's about creating a cohesive unit that can effectively collaborate, adapt to challenges, and drive the company forward.

Statistics reveal that up to 90% of startups fail. While various factors contribute to this, three key reasons stand out:

1. **Product Market Fit:** The product doesn't address a real need or solves a problem in a way that resonates with the target audience.
2. **Investment Gaps:** Inability to secure sufficient funding can cripple a startup's growth potential.
3. **Team Ineffectiveness:** Lack of talent, poor team dynamics, or inadequate leadership can hinder progress and lead to failure.

It's important to note that the team plays a crucial role in addressing the other two factors. A strong team can identify market opportunities, build a compelling value proposition, and attract investors.

Key Steps:

1. Define Clear Responsibilities:
- Forget generic job titles. Define each role's specific responsibilities and desired outcomes.
- Map out the customer journey and identify the key tasks required at each stage.
- Assign roles based on individual strengths and expertise.

2. Identify Critical Roles:
- Not all roles are created equal. Identify the most crucial positions that directly impact the product's success.
- In a tech startup, the software developer might be the most critical role.

3. Look for Past Achievements:
- During interviews, focus on past experiences where candidates played a pivotal role in achieving success.
- Listen for stories where they say, "This wouldn't have been possible without me."

4. Seek Complementary Skills:
- Look for partners who bridge your gaps and possess skills you lack.
- Avoid hiring clones of yourself. Diversity in thought and expertise leads to better problem-solving and innovation.

5. Value Hands-On Doers:
- Be wary of individuals who talk a big game but lack action.

- Look for individuals with a proven track record of hard work and dedication.

6. Passion is Key:
- Hire people who are passionate about what they do.
- Passion fuels intrinsic motivation and drives individuals to excel.

7. Respect for the Target Audience:
- Ensure your team respects and values the customer base you serve.
- No company can thrive with individuals who disrespect their target audience.

8. Invest in Team Potential:
- Smart investors often prioritize the team over the idea or product.
- They invest in individuals they believe can adapt, overcome challenges, and drive the company forward.

9. Protect Your Budget:
- Hire people for current needs & responsibilities
- Think carefully about investing for future responsibilities
- Roll up your sleeves and take on multiple responsibilities and motivate your recruits to do the same

10. Define Your Purpose and Values:
- Clearly articulate your company's mission, vision, and core values. These will guide your team and attract individuals aligned with your goals.

- Create a "*Massive Transformative Purpose*" (MTP) that inspires and motivates your team to achieve something bigger than themselves.

Creating a *Massive Transformative Purpose (MTP)* that inspires and motivates your team is a critical step in building a successful and meaningful organization.

Here's how you can do it:

1. Start with introspection:
   - Reflect on your own values and aspirations. What drives you? What legacy do you want to leave behind?
   - Consider the current state of the world. What are the biggest challenges and opportunities facing humanity?
   - Imagine a better future. What does it look like? What role do you and your organization play in making it happen?
2. Define your core beliefs:
   - Identify the fundamental principles that guide your organization's decisions and actions. These beliefs should be authentic, meaningful, and aspirational.
   - Articulate your unique value proposition. What makes your organization different? How will you make a lasting impact on the world?
3. Craft your MTP statement:
   - Use clear, concise, and inspiring language. Focus on the positive impact you want to create.
   - Make it specific enough to be actionable, but broad enough to encompass a wide range of possibilities.
   - Ensure it resonates with your team members and elicits a sense of excitement and commitment.
4. Share and activate your MTP:

- Communicate your MTP clearly and consistently to your entire team.
- Integrate your MTP into your company culture, values, and everyday decisions.
- Create opportunities for your team members to contribute to achieving your MTP.
- Celebrate successes and milestones along the way.

5. Continuously refine and evolve your MTP:
   - Be open to feedback and adapt your MTP as your organization and the world around you change.
   - Regularly revisit your MTP to ensure it remains relevant and inspiring.

Tips:
- Think big and audacious. Don't be afraid to dream big and set ambitious goals.
- Focus on the positive. Your MTP should inspire hope and optimism for the future.
- Make it personal. Connect your MTP to the values and aspirations of your team members.
- Use storytelling. Share stories of individuals and organizations making a difference in the world.
- Be authentic and genuine. Your team can spot insincerity a mile away.

Building a strong team is just the first step on the path to success.

While talented individuals can achieve great things, their collaboration often throws up unexpected challenges. To ensure your team thrives, it's crucial to be prepared for these potential roadblocks.

Effective team management is an ongoing process that requires constant evaluation, adaptation, and investment.

1. Delegate effectively: Clearly define roles, responsibilities, and expectations for each team member. Empower them with ownership and decision-making authority within their domains.
2. Foster open communication: Encourage open dialogue and feedback loops. Implement communication channels and tools that facilitate information flow and collaboration.
3. Set clear goals and expectations: Establish measurable goals aligned with your overall business objectives. Provide regular feedback and track progress against these goals to ensure team alignment and motivation.
4. Promote continuous learning and development: Invest in training programs, workshops, and mentoring opportunities to help your team develop new skills and stay up-to-date with industry trends.
5. Recognize and reward achievements: Celebrate successes and milestones to boost morale and encourage continued effort. Implement performance management systems that provide fair compensation and recognition based on individual contributions.
6. Address conflict constructively: Develop conflict resolution strategies and tools to address disagreements and maintain a positive team environment.
7. Prioritize well-being: Encourage healthy work-life balance and promote initiatives that support employee mental and physical health.
8. Conduct regular team evaluations: Regularly assess team performance and dynamics. Identify areas for

improvement and adjust your management approach based on your findings.
9. Lead by example: Be a role model for your team by demonstrating the values and behaviors you expect from them. Be transparent in your communication and hold yourself accountable.
10. Embrace agility and adapt: Be prepared to adjust your team structure and management approach as your business needs evolve. Embrace change and encourage a culture of continuous improvement.

Anticipate the roadblocks:
- Personality clashes: Diverse perspectives are valuable, but they can also lead to friction. Be prepared to mediate conflicts and foster respectful communication.
- Communication breakdowns: Lack of clarity and transparency can lead to confusion and inefficiency. Implement clear communication channels and encourage open dialogue.
- Unrealistic expectations: Unclear goals and timelines can demotivate and disillusion your team. Set realistic expectations and provide regular feedback to keep everyone on track.
- Lack of ownership: Without feeling invested in the project, team members may become disengaged and unproductive. Foster a sense of ownership by delegating tasks effectively and encouraging individual contributions.
- Burnout: Long hours and high workloads can lead to mental and physical exhaustion. Promote a healthy work-life balance and encourage team members to prioritize their well-being.

Prepare for the challenges:
- Invest in team building: Activities and workshops can help build trust, improve communication, and strengthen team dynamics.
- Develop conflict resolution skills: Equip your team with the tools and techniques to resolve disagreements constructively.
- Implement clear communication protocols: Establish well-defined channels for information sharing and feedback loops to ensure everyone is aligned.
- Foster a culture of transparency: Be open and honest in your communication, and encourage team members to voice their concerns and ideas.
- Promote a supportive environment: Create a space where team members feel comfortable asking for help and sharing their struggles.
- Recognize and reward accomplishments: Celebrating successes, both big and small, boosts morale and motivates continued effort.

By anticipating potential problems and proactively preparing for them, you can navigate the complexities of teamwork and create an environment where your talented team can thrive and achieve extraordinary results.

Thought-Provoking Questions:

1. What makes your product a market leader? Identifying this unique selling point helps you find the essential roles within your team.
2. Why can't I find the "perfect" employee? Rethink your approach. Are you offering a compelling work

environment? Are you focusing solely on cost and neglecting other important factors?
3. How can we improve? Continuously assess your team's strengths and weaknesses. Are there areas where expertise is lacking?
4. Who should I assign this task to? Avoid redundancy. Hire individuals with diverse skill sets to maximize efficiency.
5. How do I find creative talent? Foster a culture of open communication and encourage innovative thinking. Embrace and reward good ideas, even if they come with initial flaws.
6. How do I motivate my employees? Offer incentives beyond just a salary. Consider partnerships, equity sharing, or inspiring them with your vision for the future.
7. What should I do with underperforming employees? Holding onto individuals who aren't contributing is detrimental to the company's success. Consider providing support and training, or making difficult decisions if necessary.

Continuously invest in your people, provide opportunities for growth, and foster a positive and collaborative work environment. By doing so, you'll create a foundation for sustainable success and reach new heights with your startup.

Inspiring Business Tales:

* **WhatsApp's Lean and Focused Team**
WhatsApp, co-founded by Brian Acton and Jan Koum, maintained a small but highly skilled team even as its user base rapidly expanded. The startup famously had only 55 employees when it was acquired by Facebook for $19 billion. The focus was on hiring only essential personnel who were highly skilled and could manage multiple roles, ensuring agility and efficiency. This lean team approach allowed WhatsApp to remain nimble and focused, key factors in its massive growth and popularity.

* **Dropbox's Creative Recruitment Strategy**
In its early days, Dropbox faced challenges in hiring top talent due to competition from larger companies. To overcome this, they turned to creative methods to showcase their culture and attract candidates. One notable example was their use of a unique recruitment video that went viral. The video highlighted Dropbox's culture and the exciting technical challenges the team was tackling, drawing interest from top engineers. This out-of-the-box recruitment strategy helped Dropbox attract high-caliber talent, crucial for its growth and development.

* **HubSpot's Culture of Transparency and Learning**
HubSpot, a leader in inbound marketing and sales software, focused on creating a culture of transparency and continuous learning to attract and retain top talent. They implemented practices like publishing their culture code online, which detailed their values and operating principles, and offered employees numerous opportunities for growth and development. This transparent and nurturing environment

helped HubSpot build a highly skilled and loyal team, contributing significantly to its rapid growth and success.

✴ **Buffer's Emphasis on Open Salaries**

Social media management tool Buffer took a highly unusual approach by making salaries completely transparent within the company. They also adopted a formula for determining pay, which was based on role, experience, and location. This level of transparency aimed to build trust and fairness within the team. Buffer's approach to open salaries and transparency has attracted individuals who value honesty and openness, fostering a strong and cohesive team culture.

✴ **GitLab's All-Remote Team**

GitLab, the DevOps platform, is notable for its all-remote team, with employees spread across various countries and time zones. GitLab's focus has been on building a strong remote work culture with an emphasis on communication, flexibility, and trust. This model has allowed GitLab to tap into a global talent pool and build a diverse and efficient team, setting a standard for remote work practices.

✴ **Basecamp's Emphasis on Work-Life Balance**

Project management tool Basecamp has built its team with a strong emphasis on work-life balance, including a 4-day workweek during summer months and allowing remote work. These policies have helped Basecamp attract talent seeking a more balanced and flexible work environment, contributing to high employee satisfaction and retention. This approach has proven that productivity can be maintained with a more balanced work schedule, challenging traditional work norms.

* **Color Labs' Internal Conflicts**
Color Labs, a photo-sharing and social networking app, raised $41 million before its launch. However, it failed within a year of operation. Internal conflicts among team members, including disagreements between the CEO and the rest of the team, were a significant factor. This lack of cohesion and clear leadership direction ultimately led to the startup's downfall.

* **Webvan's Overambitious Expansion**
Webvan, an online grocery delivery service, was one of the most notable failures of the dot-com bubble era. While multiple factors contributed to Webvan's failure, one key aspect was its management team's decision to expand rapidly without a sustainable business model. This overambitious expansion, driven by the team's lack of experience in the grocery industry, led to enormous costs and ultimately the company's bankruptcy.

> **"Your job as CEO of a startup is to assemble a team that truly enjoys working together building a product they truly believe needs to exist."**
>
> **— Andrew Gazdecki**

2 – How to Build a Minimum Viable Product

The allure of creating the perfect product, packed with every imaginable feature, can be a seductive trap.

While ambition is a valuable trait, it can lead to what we call "feature creep," ultimately hindering your product's success.

We will guide you through the crucial process of building a Minimum Viable Product (MVP) and avoid the pitfalls of feature overload.

Imagine pouring your heart and soul into crafting a meticulously detailed product, only to find minimal market traction.

This scenario is all too common when we prioritize comprehensive features over immediate user feedback.

Remember, infinite resources exist only in theory.

Embracing the concept of an MVP allows you to launch a product with essential functionalities while remaining flexible and adaptable to real-world user needs.

We have to face with reality: prioritization and sacrifice.

Let's be honest, parting with those meticulously curated features hurts. But consider this: the sooner you release your MVP, the sooner you gain invaluable insights into user behavior.

This feedback loop allows you to refine your product based on actual needs, not just theoretical assumptions.

Key Steps:

1. Market Validation: Before diving headfirst into development, validate your business idea through market research.
2. Feature Brainstorming: List all features your ideal product would possess.
3. Prioritization: Categorize features as "must-have", "nice-to-have", and "later".
4. Brutal Honesty: Analyze "nice-to-have" features and eliminate those that don't contribute to the core user experience or value proposition.
5. Resource Optimization: Explore ways to implement "must-have" features using minimal resources (time, money, expertise).
6. Team Collaboration: Involve key team members in the decision-making process to leverage their expertise and refine the "to-do list."
7. Timeboxing: Prioritize features based on importance and estimated development time. Include a two-week testing period for each feature to ensure functionality.
8. Set Limits: Establish a realistic deadline, ideally within 3 months, to maintain focus and prevent procrastination.
9. Schedule Development: Fit prioritized features within the set timeframe, including tasks that can be completed simultaneously.

10. **Transparency and Accountability:** Share a detailed timeline with your team, utilizing tools like Gantt charts. This shared vision serves as a commitment to delivering the MVP.

Thought-Provoking Questions:

1. What is the ONE action users must take to achieve their primary goal? This defines your core feature.
2. For each additional feature, explain how it directly benefits users and addresses a specific pain point. Consider:
   - Would users feel the job wasn't finished without this feature?
   - Does it solve a significant problem or frustration they face?
3. Define a clear success metric for each feature. Aim for 100% utilization in the first version. This could be:
   - A specific percentage of users engaging with the feature.
   - A measurable impact on user behavior (e.g., increased conversion rates).
4. Minimize the risk of missing crucial features by actively collecting user feedback:
   - Ask users "What was missing?" after they use the MVP.
   - Monitor user feedback channels for recurring pain points.
5. Focus the initial version on your most valuable customer profile:
   - This persona has a specific profession, set of needs, and challenges.

- You can address the needs of other profiles in subsequent versions.
6. Don't panic if you chose the wrong customer profile:
   - You can refine your target audience in later iterations.
   - This requires sufficient resources (time, money) for further development.
7. What is the minimum amount of data you need to validate your key assumptions?
   - Prioritize gathering data that confirms or disproves your core beliefs about your users and market.
   - This might involve user surveys, usability testing, or even basic analytics tracking.
8. How can you leverage existing tools and resources to build your MVP faster and cheaper?
   - Consider using open-source libraries, APIs, or even no-code platforms to accelerate development.
   - Every corner cut on resources allows you to launch sooner and gather valuable user feedback.
9. How can you leverage your MVP to attract potential partners or investors?
   - Showcase the early traction and positive user feedback you've received to secure funding for further development and expansion.
10. How can you build a feedback loop into your MVP to continuously learn and iterate?
    - Integrate user feedback forms, in-app surveys, or even live chat features to gather ongoing insights and continuously improve your product.

By embracing the MVP approach, you move from assumptions to reality, building a product that resonates with your target audience and adapts to their evolving needs.

Inspiring Business Tales:

✴ **Dropbox:**
The founders created a simple video explaining their file-sharing solution, demonstrating its value proposition without developing a single line of code. This 3-minute video garnered 75,000 signups overnight, proving the market demand and propelling Dropbox to become a multi-billion dollar company.

✴ **Zappos:**
The founder started by taking pictures of shoes in local stores and selling them online. This "inventory-less" approach allowed him to validate the concept of online shoe shopping without the risk of holding physical inventory. This MVP soon transformed into a thriving e-commerce giant.

✴ **UserTesting:**
This company saw a gap in the market for affordable and accessible user testing tools. Their MVP was a simple website where users could record themselves using a website or app, providing valuable feedback to developers. This low-cost solution quickly gained traction and UserTesting is now used by companies like Google, Microsoft, and Amazon.

✴ **Duolingo:**
This language learning app started with a simple mission: to make learning a new language free and fun. Their MVP

focused on gamified learning with bite-sized lessons and a focus on practical conversation skills. This engaging approach resonated with users of all ages and backgrounds, and Duolingo is now one of the most popular language learning apps globally.

"Perfectionism is a disease. Procrastination is a disease. Action is the cure."

— Richie Norton

3 – Crafting User Flows that Flow

Imagine a customer effortlessly navigating towards their goal, unhindered by obstacles or delays.

This is the essence of *"flow"*, a fundamental concept in product design.

Just as nature strives for effortless movement, your user flows should be natural, spontaneous, and effortless.

Why does flow occur so seamlessly in nature? The answer lies in the perfect harmony between the flowing element and its environment.

In business, the flow is the customer, and your product is the environment. The closer their alignment, the greater your success.

Crafting effective user flows requires a deep understanding of both your product and your users.

Key Steps:

1. Before diving into user flows, determine your product's features.
2. Map User Actions: Consider each feature individually, imagining the actions and encounters users will have while using it.

3. Charting the Path: To complete the flow, analyze the decisions and steps users must take. Think of user flows as a map of all possible decision points.
4. Tools for Collaboration: Utilize tools like Flowmapp to simplify the process and collaborate with your team on user flow revisions.
5. Expertise Matters: While drawing flows is straightforward, designing them to be optimal, efficient, and frictionless requires expertise. Consider engaging a user experience design specialist for guidance.
6. Aligning Objectives: Ensure both user objectives and product's business objectives are incorporated in the path.
7. Navigating a Digital City: Imagine your product as a city. Each feature is a building. Users don't need every building at once. Drawing the shortest path between their target building and their current location is creating "flow."
8. Guiding Users: Prioritize certain buildings (features) by widening access roads (navigation elements), increasing directional signs, or even exaggerating their size. This emphasis reflects the importance of each feature to your business.
9. Different Paths for Different Journeys: Users arrive through various channels, each with its own dynamics. For example, the homepage for someone searching on Google should differ from the one a user encounters while browsing Facebook.
10. Diverse User Experiences: Create separate user flows for different user types. For instance, Uber has distinct experiences for taxi seekers and drivers.

Thought-Provoking Questions:

1. What are the emotional undercurrents driving user behavior at different points in the flow?
2. How can I leverage user expectations and mental models to create a more intuitive experience?
3. What are the potential points of friction or confusion users might encounter? How can I mitigate them?
4. Can I leverage microinteractions to create moments of delight and surprise throughout the flow?
5. How can I personalize the flow to cater to different user types and preferences?
6. What data points can I track to identify areas for improvement and refine the flow over time?
7. How can I utilize storytelling or gamification elements to increase engagement and motivation within the flow?
8. Can I leverage accessibility best practices to ensure the flow is inclusive and usable for everyone?
9. How can I empower users with control and agency over their experience within the flow?
10. What are the ethical implications of the choices I make when designing the user flow?

With understanding and implementing these principles, you can unlock the power of user flows, creating an experience that is not just functional, but also delightful and intuitive.

The key is to ensure harmony between your product and your customers, allowing them to move seamlessly towards their goals.

Inspiring Business Tales:

* **Snapchat's Redesign Backlash (2018):**
Snapchat's redesign aimed to simplify the app's interface but faced severe criticism from users. The abrupt changes led to confusion, and many users found it less intuitive, resulting in a significant drop in user engagement.

* **Uber's "180 Days of Change" (2017):**
Uber attempted a major overhaul of its driver and rider app interfaces with the "180 Days of Change" initiative. However, the rapid changes confused drivers, affecting their earnings and satisfaction. Uber had to backtrack on some of the modifications.

* **Windows 8 Interface (2012):**
Microsoft's attempt to introduce a touch-centric interface in Windows 8 for both desktop and tablet users received mixed reactions. The dual interface design created confusion, especially for traditional desktop users, impacting the initial adoption of the operating system.

* **Digg's Version 4 Launch (2010):**
Digg, a popular social news platform, faced a user revolt after a major redesign (Version 4) that changed the platform's core features. Users found it less user-friendly, and many migrated to other platforms, contributing to Digg's decline.

* **Google Wave (2009-2010):**
Google Wave aimed to revolutionize communication and collaboration but struggled due to a complex and unclear user interface. Users found it challenging to understand the

platform's purpose and use, contributing to its eventual discontinuation.

✳ **Juicero's High-End Juicer (2017):**
Juicero faced criticism for its expensive juicing machine with a complex user flow. Users discovered that the machine wasn't necessary, as they could achieve the same result by squeezing the juice packs with their hands, leading to the company's downfall.

✳ **Theranos' MiniLab Interface (2015):**
Theranos, a health tech startup, faced usability issues with its MiniLab device interface. The complex design made it challenging for healthcare professionals to use the device effectively, adding to the company's overall troubles.

✳ **Quibi's Landscape-Only Content (2020):**
Quibi, a short-form video platform, launched with content optimized for landscape mode only. Users found this restriction inconvenient, especially for a mobile-focused platform, contributing to its eventual shutdown.

✳ **Facebook's Beacon Feature (2007):**
Facebook's Beacon feature automatically shared users' online purchases, causing privacy concerns. The lack of clear user consent and control over shared information led to a backlash, and Facebook eventually had to modify the feature.

"If we want users to like our software, we should design it to behave like a likeable person: respectful, generous and helpful."

– Alan Cooper

4 – Wireframing: More than Just Sketches

Behind every successful product is a foundation of meticulously crafted screens, each refined through countless iterations.

These early sketches, known as wireframes in the world of product development, serve a crucial purpose: they define the product's structure and functionality.

Think of a wireframe as the skeleton upon which a product is built. It provides a clear outline of the content, features, and navigation flow, ensuring a seamless user experience. Without this foundational blueprint, developers would be lost in a sea of possibilities, struggling to ensure a cohesive and intuitive user journey.

A well-designed wireframe acts as the catalyst for a chain reaction of success: it transforms into a user-centric design, which ultimately translates into a high-quality product, satisfied customers, and significant revenue.

Key Steps:

1. Define Your Product Vision: Before diving into the details, take a step back and define your product's core purpose, target audience, and key features. This will guide your wireframing decisions and ensure your design aligns with your overall vision.

2. Identify Core Features: Define the essential functionalities for the product's initial version.
3. Craft User Flows: Map out the user journey, outlining how users will interact with different features.
4. Map Your Screens: Based on the user flows, determine the necessary screens and create a sitemap.
5. Leverage Design Tools: Utilize platforms like Marvel or Whimsical to streamline the wireframing process.
6. Prioritize Usability: Focus on creating a smooth and intuitive user experience, not just aesthetics.
7. Prototype for Clarity: Use tools like InVision to create interactive prototypes that test the user experience.
8. Gather Internal Feedback: Have teammates test the prototype, identifying potential issues and refining the design.
9. Use consistent visual elements for navigation and hierarchy. Pay attention to mobile responsiveness and accessibility considerations.
10. Refine and Iterate: Based on feedback from development team, iterate on the wireframe, ensuring it addresses their needs and optimizes the user experience.

Thought-Provoking Questions:

1. What is the primary goal this wireframe aims to achieve? Is it to inform, persuade, entertain, or something else?
2. What are the user's biggest pain points and how can the wireframe address them?
3. What is the emotional context of the user when they encounter this wireframe?

4. How can the wireframe utilize white space effectively to guide user attention and prioritize information?
5. What are the alternative user journeys and how can the wireframe accommodate them?
6. How can the wireframe encourage engagement and interaction beyond passive consumption?
7. What are the ethical implications of the proposed design and user experience?
8. How can the wireframe be seamlessly integrated into the existing ecosystem (app, website, etc.)?
9. What are the opportunities for future iterations and improvements based on user data and analytics?
10. How can the wireframe be designed for accessibility and inclusivity for diverse users?

Following these steps and prioritizing user-centric design principles, you can create wireframes that form the foundation for successful and beloved products.

Functionality is just one piece of the puzzle; the key is to build a product that users enjoy and find intuitive.

"Designing a product is designing a relationship."

— Steve Rogers

5 – How to Create Impactful UX & UI

Design is more than just pleasing the eye; it's about creating a powerful impression of meticulous expertise.

This intricate field requires dedication and specialized knowledge, making it a domain best entrusted to experienced professionals. While the notion of "DIY design" might be alluring, true design mastery lies in the hands of trained professionals.

Often, design is mistakenly perceived as solely about aesthetics or visual beauty. However, its true essence lies in shaping the user's perception.

It's the point of first contact with your audience, where every detail, from layout to visual elements, transmits a subconscious message. This "first impression" design plays a crucial role in user engagement and brand perception.

Functionality, often overlooked, forms the backbone of effective design.

The existence of an entire field dedicated to it - User Experience (UX) Design - underscores its importance. Functionality ensures a product is intuitive, easy to use, and fulfills its intended purpose.

Key Steps:

1. Wireframing: Sketch out the product's basic structure and functionality.
2. Competitive Analysis: Research and understand your competitor's design choices.
3. Inspiration: Leverage design platforms like Dribbble and Behance for inspiration.
4. Utilize Resources: Explore free vector design templates and adapt them to your needs.
5. Prioritize Functionality: When faced with a choice between aesthetics and functionality, always prioritize the latter.
6. Simplicity is Key: Aim for clean and minimalist design, avoiding unnecessary details and visual clutter.
7. Consistency is King: Establish a consistent standard for sizes, fonts, headings, and spacing across the entire product.
8. Mobile-first: Design for small screens first, then consider larger displays.
9. Color with Purpose: Select a strategic color palette that reflects your brand identity. Research the psychology behind colors to maximize impact.
10. Measure and Adapt: Continuously monitor user behavior and analyze the effectiveness of various design elements, allowing for data-driven improvements.

Thought-Provoking Questions:

1. What is the primary objective of this wireframe? Is it to inform, persuade, entertain, or something else entirely? Clearly defining the objective will guide all subsequent design decisions.
2. Who is my target audience? Understanding their needs, behaviors, and expectations is crucial for crafting a relevant and user-friendly experience.
3. What information needs to be conveyed? Prioritize the most essential elements and ensure they are readily accessible and visually prominent.
4. How can I simplify the user journey? Eliminate unnecessary steps and optimize workflows for effortless navigation and interaction.
5. What are the potential pain points for users? Proactively identify and address them through intuitive design solutions.
6. How can I leverage white space effectively? Strategic use of white space can enhance clarity, improve legibility, and guide user focus.
7. Are the interactions intuitive and discoverable? Users should be able to easily understand how to interact with different elements on the screen.
8. How can I incorporate visual cues to guide user attention? Use hierarchy, color, and other visual elements to direct the user's gaze towards key information.
9. Is my wireframe responsive and adaptable to different devices? Ensure a seamless user experience across various screen sizes and platforms.

10. How does my wireframe align with the overall brand identity? Maintain consistency in tone, voice, and visual style across all touchpoints.

Ultimately, design transcends mere aesthetics. It's a powerful tool for shaping perception, building trust, and delivering a seamless user experience.

By understanding its core principles and entrusting it to professionals, you can unlock the true potential of design and create products that resonate with your audience.

> *"Want your users to fall in love with your designs? Fall in love with your users."*
>
> *— Dana Chisnell*

6 – Birthing a Brand: Perfect-Fit Product Naming

Choosing a name for something that will grow and evolve alongside you, like a child, deserves careful consideration and a touch of creativity.

Just as your business model should be unique and impactful, the name you choose for your product should be equally inspired.

Think of the first impression a name makes. It's the initial sound, the visual image it conjures, and the emotions it evokes. Your chosen title should encapsulate the feelings you want customers to experience when they encounter your product for the first time.

Key Steps:

1. Define Your Essence:
   - Identify the core values and benefits your product offers. What makes it unique and valuable?
   - Capture the essence of your product in a few descriptive words or phrases.

2. Brainstorm and Explore:
   - Engage in freewheeling brainstorming sessions with a diverse group of individuals.
   - Explore various naming strategies: descriptive, evocative, invented words, puns, etc.

- Utilize online tools like Namelix and Thesaurus.com for inspiration.

3. Prioritize Clarity and Memorability:
   - Choose a name that is easy to pronounce and understand.
   - Aim for conciseness, ideally under 22 characters for optimal impact.
   - Ensure it rolls off the tongue and is easy to remember.

4. Embrace Uniqueness and Differentiation:
   - Avoid names that are generic or easily confused with existing brands.
   - Opt for a name that stands out from the competition and grabs attention.
   - Consider using a unique spelling or wordplay to enhance memorability.

5. Consider Future Growth:
   - Avoid overly specific names that might limit your future expansion.
   - Opt for broader terms that encompass potential growth and diversification.
   - Think beyond your current product line and envision future possibilities.

6. Utilize Online Tools and Resources:
   - Check domain name availability using tools like Namemesh and Bustaname.
   - Explore social media platforms like Twitter and Instagram to see if the name is already in use.
   - Leverage online trademark databases to ensure your chosen name is unique and protected.

7. Gather Feedback and Insights:
   - Share your shortlisted names with trusted customers, potential customers, and industry experts.
   - Gather feedback on their perception of each name and its association with your product.
   - Use their insights to refine your shortlist and identify the most promising options.

8. Let Time Be Your Guide:
   - Don't rush the process. Allow time for ideas to marinate and revisit your shortlist over several days.
   - Sleep on it! Sometimes, the best solutions emerge after giving your mind time to process and refine.

9. Test and Validate:
   - Conduct A/B testing with your shortlisted names to measure customer preference.
   - Use online surveys and polls to gather further data and insights.
   - Validate your choice by testing it on real customers and target audiences.

10. Embrace the Power of Iteration: Remember, naming is a continuous process. Be open to evolving and adapting your chosen name as your product and brand grow.

Thought-Provoking Questions:

1. If your creation had a voice, what would it call itself?
2. What emotions do you want people to feel when they hear the name?

3. Would this name still be relevant in 10 years? In 50 years?
4. What sound does the name make? Is it pleasing to the ear?
5. Does the name translate well across different languages and cultures?
6. Could the name be easily mispronounced or misspelled?
7. Is the name associated with any negative connotations or meanings?
8. Is the name search engine optimized (SEO) friendly?
9. How does the name pair with your brand and visual identity?
10. Does the name spark curiosity and intrigue, inviting people to learn more?

Don't be afraid to revisit your initial decisions and make adjustments based on new information and feedback.

By following these steps and employing a touch of creativity, you'll be well on your way to finding the perfect name for your product, one that captures its essence, resonates with your customers, and stands the test of time.

7 – MVP: The Antidote to Perfection Paralysis

Every project starts with an aspiration for perfection. However, the reality of development often necessitates adjustments and pivots.

Instead of focusing on a flawless ideal, it's crucial to embrace the concept of a Minimum Viable Product (MVP).

An MVP is the initial, lean version of your product. It prioritizes core functionalities and delivers value to users quickly, with minimal resources.

This approach allows you to gather valuable user feedback, test ideas with real customers, and refine your vision before committing significant time and investment.

Benefits of an MVP:

- Rapid feedback: Get real-time user insights to inform future development cycles.
- Reduced risk: Minimize investment before validating your concept.
- Faster time to market: Deliver value to users quickly and gain traction.
- Flexibility and adaptability: Easily adjust and improve your product based on user feedback.

Key Steps:

1. Define your vision: Clearly articulate your goals and target audience.
2. Prioritize features: Identify the core functionalities necessary for initial delivery.
3. Design efficiently: Ensure a user-friendly and intuitive interface.
4. Plan strategically: Develop a roadmap with realistic timelines and milestones.
5. Embrace Agile principles: Be flexible and adaptable to changing needs.
6. Communicate effectively: Foster clear and transparent communication within your team.
7. Track progress regularly: Monitor progress and address challenges promptly.
8. Emphasize teamwork: Build a strong and collaborative team environment.
9. Nurture a positive culture: Foster a sense of ownership and shared responsibility.
10. Be prepared to compromise: Adapt your vision based on valuable insights.

Thought-Provoking Questions:

1. If our MVP fails, what will we learn, and how will it impact our future strategy?
2. Are we focusing too much on features and not enough on user experience and value creation?
3. Are we blindly following industry trends or are we innovating and addressing real user needs?

4. Are there alternative approaches to solving the problem that we haven't considered?
5. Could we leverage existing technology or platforms to build our MVP faster and more efficiently?
6. What would happen if we completely flipped our core assumptions about the product and target audience?
7. Are we comfortable with the unknown and the potential for failure, or are we clinging to a fixed vision?
8. How can we create a culture of experimentation and learning within our team?
9. Are we prepared to pivot and change direction significantly based on user feedback and market response?
10. Is our team diverse and courageous enough to challenge the status quo and embrace creative solutions?

MVP is not an end product but a stepping stone on the path to success. You can develop a product that genuinely resonates with your users and provides enduring value, by adopting this iterative approach.

8 – Unlock Customer Satisfaction with User Testing

Customers are the lifeblood of any business, and their satisfaction is paramount.

But how can we ensure our products truly meet their needs and expectations? User testing provides the crucial insights necessary to bridge the gap between design and reality.

Imagine a simple test revealing nearly 100% of the issues hindering your sales, sign-ups, and conversions.

User testing makes this a reality, exposing hidden obstacles that users face when interacting with your product.

These insights are invaluable for identifying areas for improvement, leading to increased customer satisfaction, reduced support needs, and significant cost savings in design and development.

Key Steps:

1. Ensure a Solid Foundation:
Before diving into testing, ensure your product is fully functional and features all planned functionalities for the initial phase.

2. Mapping the User Journey:
Create a detailed spreadsheet mapping every user interaction point, including:

- Test Number: For quick reference to specific test steps.
- Screen Name: Identifying the relevant screen for each step.
- Test Name: A concise description of the user action being tested.
- Steps: A clear and sequential breakdown of the user action.
- Expected Result: Defining the anticipated outcome of the action.
- Finding: Recording any unexpected or observed behavior.
- Finding Type: Categorizing findings as "Error," "Revision," or "New Development."
- Error: Requires immediate correction.
- Revision: Refers to minor improvements.
- New Development: Identifies previously unaddressed needs.
- Tested By: Identifying the individual responsible for the finding.

3. Collaborate and Communicate:
Share the spreadsheet with your team to ensure complete coverage and avoid redundancies. Eliminate the "Okay, no problem" approach that can lead to missed issues.

4. Capture the Evidence:
Use tools like Loom or Awesome to record screen captures or videos of encountered errors or unexpected situations. This visual evidence facilitates clear communication and problem explanation.

5. Seeking External Feedback:
Consider utilizing platforms like UserTesting and TryMyUI to gain insights from users unfamiliar with your product before launch. This provides valuable early feedback from a fresh perspective.

6. Automating the Process:
For products with extensive testing requirements, consider implementing test automation tools like Katalon or Smartbear. This streamlines the process and reduces manual effort.

7. Resolving Errors:
Prioritize and address all identified "errors" to ensure a seamless user experience.

8. Evaluating Revisions:
Analyze "revisions" related to user experience for their criticality. If they disrupt the user flow or create confusion, revisit the design stage.

9. Prioritizing New Developments:
Defer "new development" requests to future versions unless they are crucial for user satisfaction or significantly impact the product's viability.

10. Embrace the Iterative Process:
Expect additional work to emerge during user testing, even on seemingly finalized products.

   Resist the urge to rush and compromise quality. Instead, embrace the iterative process and leverage this valuable feedback to refine your product and achieve long-term success.

Unlocking customer satisfaction and business growth starts with user testing. By systematically incorporating user insights into your development process, you'll create a product that truly resonates with your customers, leading to loyalty and ultimately, business success.

Your customers are the heart of your product's success. Their positive experience is the key to unlocking its full potential.

Thought-Provoking Questions:

1. What are the user's mental models? How do they expect the product to work based on their existing knowledge and experiences?
2. What are the emotional triggers throughout the user journey? Where do they feel frustrated, confused, or delighted?
3. What are the user's hidden needs and desires? What are they not explicitly saying but are hoping to achieve with the product?
4. How does the user's environment and context influence their interaction with the product? Are they using it on a desktop, mobile device, or in a specific physical space?
5. What are the cultural and accessibility considerations for the user? Does the language, design, or functionality pose any barriers?

6. How does the user's technical expertise impact their experience? Are they tech-savvy or novices? How does this influence their learning curve?
7. How does the user's trust in the brand affect their perception of the product? What are their existing expectations and biases?
8. What are the user's alternative solutions or workarounds? How are they currently achieving their goals without your product?
9. What are the unintended consequences of the product's design? Are there any hidden features or functionalities that users are not aware of?
10. How can we test for the "unknown unknowns"? How can we design our user testing process to uncover unexpected and unforeseen problems?

> *"Do not seek praise. Seek criticism."*
>
> *- Paul Arden*

9 – How to Master Post-Launch Management

While the initial spark of an idea ignites the journey, the development process is just the tip of the iceberg.

The real test lies in managing a living, evolving product after its launch. It's a continuous process demanding dedication and a proactive approach.

The 5% Myth: Don't let anyone fool you; developing the product is only a fraction of the work involved. The true marathon begins when the product meets the customer.

Each day brings new challenges and unforeseen scenarios. Without anticipating these difficulties, you risk being caught off guard and struggling to maintain control.

Extracting Operational Needs: To navigate the post-launch landscape effectively, you need to map out the product's operational needs. This proactive approach identifies potential issues and empowers you to manage them efficiently.

Key Steps:

1. Define Roles and Responsibilities: Clearly communicate individual responsibilities within the team. This transparency ensures everyone is aware of their tasks and promotes accountability.

2. Plan for the Unexpected: Develop contingency plans for potential worst-case scenarios. Assign specific roles and actions to each team member, ensuring swift and effective response in emergencies.

3. Build a Robust Customer Support System: Establish a dedicated customer support team equipped to handle inquiries and solve problems. Remember, customer support isn't just about troubleshooting; it's also about identifying opportunities for product improvement.

4. Secure Operational Funding: Ensure sufficient financial resources are available to cover ongoing operational expenses. This includes staffing, maintenance, and content creation.

5. Implement a Visual Task Management System: Utilize a physical board with post-it notes to track various work stages:

- Current Work: Ongoing tasks actively being worked on.
- Blocked Jobs: Tasks stalled due to obstacles requiring immediate attention.
- Awaiting Control: Completed tasks awaiting review or final approval.
- Finished Works: Successfully completed tasks highlighting progress and achievements.
- Waiting in Queue: Prioritized tasks awaiting their turn in the workflow.
- Things to be Scheduled: Tasks to be planned and estimated for time and resources.

6. Leverage Digital Tools: Supplement your physical board with a digital project management tool like Trello. This facilitates real-time collaboration and enhanced visibility into the overall workflow.

7. Daily Stand-up Meetings: Initiate each day with a team meeting where individuals share their progress and identify any challenges. This fosters transparency and encourages collaborative problem-solving.

8. Measure and Analyze: Define key performance indicators (KPIs) to track the product's performance and identify areas for improvement. Consider automating reports for efficient data analysis.

9. External Dependencies: Clearly communicate your daily operational needs to external suppliers and vendors who play a role in maintaining your product's success.

Thought-Provoking Questions:

1. Are your processes efficient and streamlined? Can you identify and eliminate any unnecessary steps or bottlenecks in your workflow?
2. Are you leveraging technology to automate tasks? Are there repetitive or manual tasks that could be automated to free up your team's time and resources?
3. Do you have clear metrics in place to track operational performance? Are you actively monitoring and analyzing data to identify areas for improvement and optimize efficiency?

4. Are you effectively managing your inventory and supply chain? Do you have a reliable system for tracking inventory levels and ensuring timely deliveries to avoid delays and disruptions?
5. Do you have a robust communication and collaboration system in place? Can your team easily communicate and collaborate on projects to ensure everyone is on the same page?
6. Are you effectively managing your resources? Are you allocating resources efficiently to different projects and initiatives?
7. Do you have a plan for scaling your operations? How will you adapt your processes and systems to accommodate growth and increasing demand?
8. Are you regularly reviewing and improving your operational procedures? Do you have a system for identifying and eliminating inefficiencies and continuously optimizing your operations?
9. Are you adequately managing risk? Have you identified potential operational risks and implemented mitigation strategies to minimize their impact?
10. Are you benchmarking your operations against industry best practices? Are you continuously seeking to learn from others and improve your operational efficiency?

Following these steps and embracing a proactive approach empowers you to turn a potentially daunting product launch into a well-managed journey, paving the way for ongoing success.

The journey doesn't end with launch; it's a continuous cycle of learning, adaptation, and evolution that ensures your product flourishes in the long run.

Powerful Marketing Tactics for Explosive Growth

This chapter marks the pivotal moment. With great anticipation, we enter a crucial stage in our journey: meeting our customers for the first time.

We've birthed a brilliant business idea, honed a robust commercial model, and assembled a stellar team to execute our vision. Now, we stand poised at the precipice of meeting our customers.

But where and how do we find them? What strategies will ignite sales and what alternative methods might we employ? These are the questions that fuel this chapter.

While the journey thus far has been arduous and critical, the truth remains: our customer holds the ultimate key.

For the first time, our product will face its intended audience, be it receptive or indifferent. This initial encounter, this first impression, sets the stage for our business' future, acting as a litmus test for its success.

▸ 1 – Treating Customers Individually Through Segmentation

Every customer who uses your product is unique and deserves personalized attention. That's where customer segmentation comes in.

While a new company with few customers can offer individual service, this becomes impractical and inefficient as the customer base grows.

Segmentation provides the solution. By grouping customers based on shared characteristics, you can tailor communication and marketing efforts to each segment.

Instead of a generic approach, understanding and grouping your customers leads to better feedback and increased engagement. For effective marketing, customer segmentation is not just an option, it's essential.

Key Steps:

1. Understand your customers: Research their habits and preferences.
2. Segment based on relevant characteristics:
   - Behavioral: Spending habits, product usage frequency, feature preferences, feedback.
   - Psychographic: Social class, lifestyle, values, affiliations, personality.
   - Demographics: Age, gender, marital status, income, education, occupation.
   - Geography: Location (towns, districts, countries).
3. List potential customer segments: Identify all possible groups based on the chosen characteristics.
4. To Focus on the most valuable segment create a table with the following columns:
   - Number of People
   - Average Income Level
   - Ease of Access
   - Product Relevance
   - Expertise Level (Your knowledge of the group)
5. Score each segment (1-5) on each characteristic: 1 being low, 5 being high.
6. Multiply the scores for each segment: The segment with the highest score is your primary target.
7. Track customer behavior within the product: Utilize tools like Google Analytics or Firebase.
8. Identify the most and least profitable segments: Analyze data collected through step 5.
9. Continuously update the table: Add an "Income" column and track average income per segment. This allows for ongoing adjustments based on new data.

10. Craft Personas: Build detailed profiles for each segment, including demographics, motivations, and needs.

Thought-Provoking Questions:

1. What are the hidden patterns in my customer data that I'm overlooking?
2. If I could only focus on one customer segment, which would have the biggest impact?
3. What are the emotional triggers and motivators behind my customers' choices?
4. Are there any unexpected relationships between seemingly unrelated customer characteristics?
5. How can I use segmentation to identify and address customer pain points more effectively?
6. How will my target segments evolve over time, and how can I adapt my approach accordingly?
7. Can I leverage segmentation to create personalized product recommendations and promotions?
8. What are the ethical implications of using customer data for segmentation purposes?
9. How can I measure the ROI of my segmentation efforts and identify areas for improvement?
10. What cutting-edge technologies and methodologies can I use to enhance my segmentation strategy?

By following these steps, you can effectively segment your customers and tailor your marketing efforts to each group, leading to improved customer engagement and increased profitability.

2 – Test Your Marketing Channels

Finding the right marketing channel is like chasing a mirage in the desert. One minute it's there, beckoning with promises of success, the next it's vanished, leaving you parched and frustrated.

Unlike a set-it-and-forget-it task, this process demands constant adaptation and a thirst for exploration.

Recall the explosive growth of Google AdWords in its early days? Companies revelled in its revolutionary advertising platform, reaping substantial rewards.

Fast forward to today, and the landscape has morphed dramatically. Competition has reached a fever pitch, pushing ad bids through the roof and eroding the profits that once flowed freely.

Facebook ads, once a potent tool, have followed suit, their effectiveness waning with each passing year.

This dynamic isn't confined to paid channels. The realm of SEO, once the playground of a select few with "sneaky tactics," now pulsates with millions of content creators and Google's ever-evolving ranking algorithms.

No matter your marketing prowess, identifying the right channels remains an ongoing struggle. Established channels become saturated, driving up costs and diminishing returns. So, how do you navigate this shifting landscape and emerge victorious?

Embrace the spirit of exploration and embrace continuous testing! Here's your roadmap to success:

Key Steps:

Step 1: Identify Your Golden Goose:

Start by pinpointing your most profitable and sizable customer segment. Remember, different segments respond best to different channels. Tailoring your approach is paramount.

Step 2: Chart Your Course:

The marketing landscape is vast, offering a plethora of potential avenues. Consider search engines, online marketplaces, mobile apps, blogs, social media, email, events, TV commercials, and countless others.

Step 3: Narrow Your Focus:

Instead of attempting to conquer every channel, ask yourself:

- Where do your ideal customers spend their time?
- Where are they most receptive to your message?
- Where is your target audience most concentrated?
- Where do they spend the most time?
- Which platform offers the most cost-effective reach?

Focusing on one or two channels at a time allows you to develop a deeper understanding, conduct effective testing, and optimize your message and offer for maximum impact.

Step 4: Avoid the Multitasking Trap:

Juggling multiple channels simultaneously dilutes your focus and hinders optimization. Master one before venturing into others.

Step 5: Monitor Your Investment:

Track the time and resources you dedicate to each channel. Ensure your efforts are directed towards channels yielding the most valuable results.

Step 6: Learn from the Masters:

Observe your competitors' channel usage and adapt their successful strategies to your own marketing efforts.

Step 7: Quantify Your Acquisitions:

Calculate the cost of acquiring a customer through each channel. This metric helps identify the most efficient avenues for customer acquisition.

Step 8: Measure the Lifetime Value:

Analyze the revenue generated by customers acquired through different channels. Consider lifetime value (LTV) if you have a recurring revenue model.

Step 9: Own Your Marketing Destiny:

Don't outsource crucial channel discovery to external agencies. Take ownership, actively learn, and develop your own channel expertise.

Step 10: Embrace Continuous Improvement:

Prioritize channels that offer the most cost-effective customer acquisition and continuously refine your strategies for maximum impact.

Thought-Provoking Questions:

1. What are the deeply ingrained habits and behaviors of your ideal customer? Understanding their daily routine and preferred information consumption channels can reveal hidden opportunities.
2. What emotions do you want to evoke in your audience? Choosing channels that resonate with those emotions can create a stronger connection and drive action.
3. What content format would provide the most value to your audience at each stage of the customer journey? Different channels may be better suited for different stages, like awareness, consideration, and decision-making.
4. How can you measure the effectiveness of each channel beyond vanity metrics? Look beyond clicks and impressions to metrics like conversions, revenue, and customer lifetime value.
5. What unexpected channels could offer unique opportunities to reach your target audience? Think

beyond the usual suspects and explore emerging platforms or niche communities.
6. How can you leverage technology to automate and optimize your channel testing process? Tools and platforms can help you gather data, analyze results, and make data-driven decisions faster.
7. How can you collaborate with other businesses or influencers to expand your reach through specific channels? Partnerships can expose you to new audiences and leverage complementary strengths.
8. How can you measure the long-term impact of your chosen channels on brand awareness and loyalty? Consider brand recall, customer sentiment, and repeat purchase rates.
9. What are your competitors doing on different channels? Analyze their successes and failures to inform your own strategy and identify potential gaps you can exploit.
10. How can you adapt your approach to different channels while maintaining brand consistency and messaging? Ensure your brand voice and values are reflected across all channels for a seamless customer experience.

The marketing landscape is a living, breathing entity, constantly evolving and transforming.

By embracing exploration, focusing your efforts, and learning from your data, you can navigate its shifting sands and discover the channels that propel your business forward.

3 – The Missing Ingredient in Your Marketing Strategy

Marketing experts often cloak themselves in an aura of mystique when they invoke the term "storytelling." Yet, the idea of "selling with a story" is surprisingly simple and intuitively understood.

Humans are naturally drawn to stories. Why? Because they are accessible, engaging, and follow a clear arc of beginning, middle, and satisfying end. Each story offers a journey with a desirable reward, reflecting relatable experiences and human emotions.

Jonathan Gottschall aptly observed,

> **"As humanity, we are addicted to stories. So much so that even when our body falls asleep, our mind stays up all night and tells itself stories."**

This inherent connection is why stories resonate so deeply with us.

Consider the enduring power of religious narratives. Instilling a lifelong belief system is no easy feat, yet religion accomplishes this seemingly effortlessly. The key lies in storytelling. Stories provide a lossless channel for transmitting information, allowing it to take root and flourish in the minds of others.

As an entrepreneur, building a sustainable, high-income business hinges on making your product an indispensable part of your customers' lives. They should feel incomplete without it, even if that's not strictly true. This conviction requires a compelling story.

Think of iconic brands like Apple, Nike, Starbucks, and Coca-Cola. They don't just sell products; they sell an identity, a belief system, a lifestyle. This is why their products are so desirable, even at premium prices.

The alternative is the approach adopted by 99% of businesses: buying attention on diverse marketing channels. This route requires constant anxiety and a fervent hope that your investments yield returns.

"But I don't have a story" you might lament. This is rarely true. Your story already exists, waiting to be unearthed and crafted. Together, we can embark on the journey of bringing your story to life, step by step.

Key Steps:

1. Find Your Why:

Why choose the entrepreneurial path, fraught with stress and uncertainty, when other options exist? Dive deep and ask yourself this question repeatedly. Write down your answers. By the tenth "why," you'll uncover the core of your story.

2. Share It Authentically:

No matter how unusual your story may feel, sharing it authentically will resonate with others. Customers, colleagues, and partners will connect with your genuineness, fostering empathy and trust.

3. Connecting Story and Product:

Examine your product through the lens of your story. Assess its quality, price point, and problem-solving ability. Does it fulfill a longing or differentiate itself from competitors? These answers, explored in your business model, should be woven into your narrative.

4. Cultivating a Brand Personality:

Your story should embody a distinct personality - a set of values, principles, and "no-go" zones. This personality needs to be consistently expressed across all channels and touchpoints.

5. Keep it Simple:

People lose interest quickly. Favor concise, clear messaging over lengthy explanations. Let your story be easily understood and remembered.

6. Empower Customer Storytelling:

Encourage customers to share their experiences and stories that resonate with your own. This creates a powerful community around your brand.

7. Brand Consistency:

The visual language of your brand should reflect your story. If your narrative is one of warmth and care, your visuals cannot be cold and sterile.

8. Small Gestures, Big Impact:

Show your customers you care through small, unexpected surprises. This goes a long way in building trust and strengthening your story.

9. Authenticity is Key:

Storytelling for mere sales purposes is easily detected. You must truly believe and live your own story. If it isn't genuine, it won't resonate.

10. Beyond Marketing:

Remember, Mikael Cho's words ring true:

> ***"The best marketing is when you don't realize it's marketing."***

Make your story authentic and impactful, and the marketing becomes a natural byproduct.

Thought-Provoking Questions:

1. What is the emotional core of your story? What makes your audience feel something? Joy, sadness, anger, hope - what resonates with them?
2. Who is the hero of your story? Is it you, your team, or your customers? Who embodies the journey and transformation you want to portray?
3. What are the stakes of your story? What is at risk if your hero fails? How does this raise the tension and keep your audience engaged?
4. What are the obstacles and villains in your story? What challenges does your hero face, and who or what opposes them? This creates conflict and drives the narrative forward.
5. How does your story connect with a universal human experience? Does it touch on themes of love, loss, hope, or fear? This relatability makes your story more meaningful and impactful.
6. What is the turning point in your story? When does your hero face a defining moment that changes their trajectory? This is crucial for character development and narrative tension.
7. What is the resolution of your story? Does your hero succeed or fail? How does their journey conclude, and what lessons are learned? This provides closure and leaves a lasting impression.
8. What senses are you engaging in your storytelling? How do you use vivid descriptions, evocative language, and imagery to draw your audience into your world?
9. What is the call to action in your story? What do you want your audience to do after hearing your story? This

could be anything from subscribing to your newsletter to purchasing your product.
10. Is your story authentic and true to your brand? Does it reflect your values, mission, and vision? This ensures your story resonates with your audience and builds trust.

"Twenty years ago if you provided someone with horrible service, it may take weeks or even months for the word-of-mouth message to get out to 15-20 potential customers.

Today, with social media, thousands of potential customers can learn about horrible service within hours, minutes or even seconds after it happens."

— Bill Capodagli

4 – Cultivating Loyal Fans for Your Brand

Brand ambassadors are more than just faces promoting a product; they are passionate individuals who genuinely believe in your brand and its values.

They see your creation as an extension of themselves and actively advocate for it without expecting anything in return. This type of loyalty is invaluable, allowing your company to thrive for years to come.

But how do you find these elusive individuals? Is it just a lucky draw? Not at all! This phenomenon, often referred to as "Word-of-Mouth Marketing," can be intentionally cultivated through strategic actions.

Key Steps:

1. Craft a Compelling Story: Every brand with loyal ambassadors has a unique story to tell. If your story isn't compelling, don't expect dedicated fans. Find the narrative that resonates with your audience and share it authentically.
2. Empower Your Employees: Your employees are your first line of brand ambassadors. Foster a culture of pride and engagement within your company. When employees are happy, they become natural advocates for your brand.

3. Recognize Existing Champions: You might be surprised to discover that you already have loyal ambassadors among your existing customer base. Use tools like the Net Promoter Score (NPS) to identify promoters (those who score 9-10) and actively engage with them.
4. Nurture Relationships: Show your appreciation for your ambassadors. Maintain open communication channels and provide them with exclusive content and opportunities.
5. Empower Advocacy: Instead of directly asking for recommendations, consider offering incentives like free trials or discounts for referring friends. This creates a natural opportunity for ambassadors to share their positive experiences.
6. Leverage Social Media: Connect with your ambassadors on social media and provide platforms for them to naturally promote your brand. Encourage them to share their own stories and experiences.
7. Listen and Reward: Actively monitor social media conversations about your brand. Respond to positive feedback and surprise those who are vocal about their appreciation.
8. Share User-Generated Content: Feature stories and testimonials from your ambassadors on your official channels. This showcases their genuine experiences and builds trust with potential customers.
9. While cultivating organic brand ambassadors takes time and effort, there's a shortcut: collaborating with paid influencers. However, this approach demands caution. Choose influencers who genuinely connect with your target audience and whose values align with your brand. Authentic advocacy is key to avoiding backlash and building genuine trust.

10. Ultimately, having loyal brand ambassadors boils down to one thing: creating a community.

Thought-Provoking Questions:

1. What core values does my brand embody, and how can I weave them into a compelling narrative that resonates with potential ambassadors?
2. Are my employees genuinely excited about the brand and its impact? If not, what needs to change to turn them into passionate advocates?
3. Who are my existing customers who consistently express positive feedback and share their experiences with others? How can I nurture these relationships and encourage further advocacy?
4. What are the specific behaviors and characteristics that define a "brand ambassador" for my company? How can I identify these traits in potential partners?
5. Beyond financial incentives, what motivates individuals to become vocal supporters of a brand? How can I offer value that aligns with their interests and aspirations?
6. What platforms and channels do my target audience frequent? How can I create a presence there that facilitates authentic brand engagement and advocacy opportunities?
7. How can I empower my ambassadors to share their own unique stories and experiences with my brand? What tools and resources can I provide to facilitate their efforts?
8. How can I measure the impact of my brand ambassador program? What metrics are most relevant to quantifying its success and ROI?

9. What are the potential pitfalls of using paid influencers as brand ambassadors? How can I ensure that such partnerships remain authentic and beneficial?
10. What can I learn from other successful brands in my industry regarding their approach to building a strong community of brand ambassadors? What best practices can I adapt and apply to my own strategy?

By fostering a sense of belonging and shared purpose, you can attract and retain individuals who are passionate about your brand and its mission.

"Everyone has an opinion. But the main thing is to attract thousands of people who are willing to help you spread your idea."

— Jack Dorsey

5 – Unlocking the Power of Organic Growth

Ever wondered how to attract customers without spending a dime on advertising? The answer lies in organic acquisition, where users discover your product naturally.

Think of it as leaving a trail of delicious crumbs, enticing them to explore further.

Key Steps:

1. The Secret Sauce: Stories and Advice

There are two primary ways organic discovery occurs: stories and advice. Stories captivate us, sharing experiences and emotions that resonate with our own. Advice offers valuable insights, guiding us towards solutions and knowledge.

2. Instagram: A Masterclass in Organic Growth

Instagram exemplifies how to leverage these principles seamlessly. Their design encourages photo sharing, rewarding us with "hearts" - a simple yet powerful dopamine trigger. This creates a loop: we crave validation, share photos, receive hearts, and feel happy. This cycle fuels our engagement and fuels Instagram's growth.

3. Content as a Magnet:

Create content that speaks to your target audience's interests, addressing their needs and sparking curiosity. When they discover your content in their online searches, they'll naturally gravitate towards your product.

4. Unlocking Organic Insights:

Utilize analytics tools like Google Analytics to differentiate between organic and paid customer acquisition. If direct tracking isn't feasible, conduct simple surveys asking "Where did you hear about us?"

5. Beyond the Obvious:

Once you understand your organic customer base, identify their common characteristics and explore ways to reach similar individuals. Consider advertising on platforms popular with your target audience or invest in SEO strategies to improve your search ranking.

6. Building Trust, Winning Hearts:

Encourage your happy customers to leave reviews, highlighting positive feedback. Consider sharing these testimonials to build trust and attract new users.

7. Standards, Reviews, and Approvals:

Seek industry accreditations, positive reviews, and other forms of validation. These act as social proof, convincing potential customers that you offer a valuable product.

8. Beyond Acquisition: Building Loyalty

Nir Eyal, a behavioral design expert, reminds us that

"It's much more cost-effective to retain existing customers than to find new ones."

Focus on building a loyal user base by creating a product that fosters genuine engagement and offers intrinsic rewards.

9. Community Spark:

Build a forum, host events, reward top contributors.

10. UGC Powerhouse:

Curate user content, partner with micro-influencers, incentivize creation.

Thought-Provoking Questions:

1. What story is my brand telling? How does it resonate with my target audience?

2. What unmet needs or desires does my product address? How can I amplify these benefits organically?

3. What are the "micro-habits" or recurring behaviors I can design into my product to fuel engagement and loyalty?

4. Where do my ideal customers naturally congregate online? How can I become a valuable resource within those communities?

5. What are the "dark alleys" of the internet where my target audience seeks information not readily available elsewhere? How can I illuminate those paths?

6. What unexpected collaborations could unlock new organic growth opportunities?

7. How can I leverage the power of gamification to incentivize organic customer acquisition and engagement?

8. What are the ethical considerations of organic growth strategies, and how can I ensure my approach is transparent and responsible?

9. How can I turn my happy customers into organic growth ambassadors through word-of-mouth marketing and user-generated content?

10. What are the emerging trends in organic growth, and how can I stay ahead of the curve and adapt my strategies accordingly?

   Scattering "*delicious crumbs*" of stories, advice, and valuable content attracts customers organically, building a thriving and sustainable business.

   While organic growth requires dedication and patience, the rewards are long-lasting and immensely satisfying.

6 – Leveraging Partnerships for Business Growth

Partnering with another company can be a powerful tool for expanding your customer base and achieving strategic goals. These collaborations offer multiple benefits:

- **Enhanced Customer Value:** Partnerships can enable you to deliver greater value to existing customers through complementary products or services.
- **New User Acquisition:** Reach new customers and markets through your partner's established audience.
- **Increased Sales:** Partnerships can drive sales growth through joint marketing initiatives and cross-promotion opportunities.
- **Reduced Costs:** Collaborations can help you achieve economies of scale and share resources, lowering overall costs.

To ensure a successful partnership, follow these key steps:

Key Steps:

1. **Identify Your Core Business:** Clearly define the essential aspects of your operation that set you apart from competitors.
2. **Partner for Non-Core Functions:** Consider partnering for anything outside your core business, allowing you to focus on your strengths.

3. **Identify Complementary Products:** Look for products that naturally complement your offerings and provide additional value to your customers.
4. **Partner for Efficiency:** Seek partnerships that streamline your operations and reduce costs compared to doing things alone.
5. **Leverage Sales Channels:** Partner with media outlets or platforms to reach new customers and drive sales.
6. **Build Trust through Associations:** Collaborate with respected organizations to enhance your brand reputation and build trust with customers.
7. **Partner for Cross-Promotion:** Organize campaigns to introduce your customers to complementary products and services offered by your partner.
8. **Offer Expert Services:** Sell your expertise and knowledge through consultancy models to interested companies.
9. **Expand Locally with Local Partners:** Collaborate with companies that have strong local market influence to reach new customers.
10. **Organize Industry Events:** Join forces with non-competitive companies to organize industry events that attract your ideal customers.

Thought-Provoking Questions:

1. What complementary skills or resources can other companies offer to enhance our current offerings and solve customer pain points collaboratively?
2. Instead of competing with emerging players, how can we partner with them to gain a competitive advantage and dominate the market together?

3. How can we combine our strengths with seemingly unrelated companies to create a unique value proposition that attracts new customer segments?
4. What joint marketing initiatives can we launch with unexpected partners to reach wider audiences and achieve greater brand awareness?
5. How can we leverage partnerships to co-develop innovative products or services that address emerging customer needs and disrupt the market?
6. Instead of acquiring new technology, how can we collaborate with companies who specialize in that technology to gain access and expertise?
7. How can we partner with non-profit organizations to access new markets, build trust with stakeholders, and contribute to social impact?
8. How can we create cross-industry alliances to tackle complex challenges and develop solutions that benefit both individual companies and society as a whole?
9. What collaborative innovation opportunities exist with potential competitors to advance the industry and create shared value for all stakeholders?
10. How can we reframe competition as a catalyst for collaboration, allowing us to jointly overcome industry-wide obstacles and unlock new growth opportunities?

You can effectively leverage partnerships to boost your business growth and achieve long-term success, if you implementing these strategies.

7 – Unleashing Revenue Potential

Growing a small business requires focus on both existing customers and new income streams.

Sales remain the lifeblood of any business, fueling growth and enabling investments in talent, resources, and service quality.

Key Steps:

1. First, get the most out of your marketing spend. Optimize.

2. There are four pillars of revenue growth:
   - Customer Acquisition: Expanding your customer base is paramount. Leverage effective marketing strategies that deliver maximum value for every penny spent.
   - Average Transaction Value: Increasing the amount spent per customer directly boosts revenue. Implement strategies like upselling and cross-selling.
   - Sales Efficiency: Optimize your sales force by maximizing sales per person. Equip them with the right tools and training.
   - Pricing Optimization: Analyze current pricing models and consider adjustments that reflect product value and market conditions.

3. Recommendation Engine:
Empower your customers to become brand ambassadors. Implement a system that incentivizes referrals and recommendations.

4. Global Expansion:
Explore opportunities in new markets. Adapt your product to local preferences and cultural nuances.

5. Strategic Partnerships:
Collaborate with complementary businesses to offer new products and services. Utilize a commission-based model to share profits.

6. Bulk Sales:
Identify potential bulk buyers and offer attractive deals to secure large orders.

7. Customized Campaigns:
Design targeted campaigns for different customer segments to maximize sales across your entire customer base.

8. Cost Optimization:
Analyze and reduce unit costs by identifying and eliminating unnecessary expenses.

9. Business Model Review:
Regularly revisit and refine your business model to ensure it remains relevant and adaptable.

10. Loyalty Program: Implement a loyalty program to reward and retain valuable customers, encouraging continued engagement and increased revenue.

Thought-Provoking Questions:

1. What untapped opportunities lie within our existing customer base? Can we upsell, cross-sell, or increase their purchase frequency?
2. How can we turn "just browsing" visitors into paying customers? What are the key friction points in our conversion funnel?
3. Are we effectively leveraging the power of storytelling and emotional connection in our sales approach? How can we craft a compelling narrative that resonates with our target audience?
4. What are the hidden barriers preventing customers from buying? Are they price-sensitive, concerned about risk, or lacking awareness? How can we address these concerns directly?
5. How can we leverage exclusivity, scarcity, or urgency to create a sense of desire and motivate immediate action?
6. Is our pricing strategy optimized for both value perception and profitability? Are we leaving money on the table by undercharging or overcharging?
7. How can we integrate data-driven insights into our sales process to personalize offers and maximize conversion rates?
8. Are we maximizing the potential of our existing marketing channels? Are there untapped channels we can explore to reach a wider audience?

9. How can we gamify the sales experience to drive engagement, motivation, and competition within our sales team?
10. What are the most effective incentives for motivating our sales team to achieve their targets? Are we offering the right mix of financial rewards, recognition, and personal growth opportunities?

Implementing these strategies and focusing on continuous improvement, small businesses can unlock their full revenue potential and achieve sustainable growth.

"Profit is like oxygen, food, water and blood for the body; they are not the point of life, but without them, there is no life."

— James C. Collins

8 – Optimize to Thrive: Change, Correct, Renew, Update

If you want to make it easier for your business idea to succeed, gain more customers, make more sales, and earn more money, optimize, optimize & optimize.

Your most important duty as a founder is to use your limited resources, money and time efficiently.

Entrepreneurship is the art of using limited resources with priorities that will provide the highest output.

Marketing optimization is the work of improving efficiency, where you look at marketing campaign data and decide which channels, which ads, and which campaigns will continue to run and which you should pause.

Key Steps:

1. The first step in optimization starts with choosing the right marketing channel.

2. You can gain customers and make sales by using a channel. So how do we know if it is efficient enough? By measuring.

- You should clearly know the money you spent on that channel.

- You should know the number of customers you gained thanks to that channel.
- In this way, you can calculate the acquisition cost required to gain a customer from that channel.
- You should also be able to measure the total money that the customers you earned from that channel earned you throughout all the times they used your product. When you divide this income by the total number of customers you gained from that channel, you find the income (Life Time Value) earned from an average customer coming from that channel.
- So you know the net income you earned from that channel; [AC] - [LTV]

3. All your efforts should be to increase this net income. For this, the first thing you need to do is to detail the path of the customer acquired through this marketing channel.

- How many people see the ad?
- How many show interest? (Ex: click)
- How many of those who click become members?
- How many of the members make purchases?
- How many of those who make purchases make repeat purchases?
- What is the average revenue of a sale?
- How many of the purchasers request a refund?
- What is the cost incurred by members during their average usage period?
- What is the average rate of members inviting another friend?
- On average, how long does it take for members of this channel to make purchases?

4. The first thing you will focus on is establishing a technical analysis and reporting structure where you can get clear answers to all the questions above. If you can't answer these questions clearly, you can't improve anything.

5. If you have established a structure where you can find the answers to the questions above for each marketing channel you use, the only thing you need to do is to follow day by day whichever is more efficient and brings more profit, reduce your investment in the one that earns you less, and increase your investment in the channel you earn more. That's exactly the gist of it.

6. Think of it like a funnel with holes. You pour water at the top of the funnel, but not as much water reaches the bottom as you pour from the top. Whatever you do. You spot the holes in the funnel and close them, right? This is exactly what we call optimization. What you need to do is focus on these breakdowns. By asking the following questions and finding logical solutions, the implementation process itself becomes optimization.

- How can more people see the ad?
  - Sample answer: I can advertise on more channels
- What can I do to increase the rate of clicks among those who see the ad?
  - A: I make the advertising visual more attractive. I update my slogan.
- How can I increase the rate of members among those who click?
  - A: I would make the sign up button on my website more prominent.

- How can I increase the rate of people making purchases?
  - A: I create a campaign with an unbeatable price.
- How can I increase the rate of repeat purchasers?
  - A: By adding new features to the product, ensuring that my customers are more satisfied with the product and use it for a longer time.
- ...

7. Optimization is incredibly time consuming. This means that some of your employees spend time on this and the majority of the salary you give to those employees goes to optimization, which means expense, cost. Therefore, if you improve with optimization, you should continue optimizing. You change things but if the results don't improve, you should stop immediately and try something else.

8. How will you know if the changes you make during optimization are working? By measuring, of course. We call this A/B testing.

9. There are platforms or software that will facilitate A/B testing for every digital product. Buy. If it seems expensive, you should solve this with your own software team. You should clearly know how each important change you make affects the answers to the 10 questions in the third article.

10. Marketing is, in the most general sense, a matter of trial and error. Better target audience, better price, better color, better slogan... Optimization is the work of striving to find the better one. If you do this job based on data, monitor and repeat it every day, and improve your results a

little more every day, then you are doing optimization justice.

Thought-Provoking Questions:

1. What are the core assumptions driving our current approach? Are they still valid?
2. What are the true bottlenecks impacting our efficiency and effectiveness?
3. If we could radically change one aspect of our process, what would it be and why?
4. How do the perceived benefits of optimization compare to the actual costs and effort involved?
5. Are we measuring the right metrics to track progress and identify opportunities for improvement?
6. Are we effectively leveraging data and insights to inform our optimization decisions?
7. What are the potential unintended consequences of making certain optimizations?
8. How can we ensure that optimization efforts align with our long-term strategic goals?
9. Are we fostering a culture of continuous learning and experimentation within our team?
10. How can we translate optimization successes into sustainable improvements across the organization?

"Optimization hinders evolution."
– Alan Perlis

Mastering the Challenges of Global Success

This section delves into the complexities of transforming your product into a global phenomenon.

We'll explore the potential hurdles, from adapting to diverse cultural codes to navigating the intricate world of international investors.

Some products face intricate cultural nuances, necessitating thorough research into the socio-cultural structures of each target market.

Conversely, others tap into universal human needs, allowing for swift global expansion.

The crucial questions emerge: which country serves as the ideal launchpad? How will our strategy evolve across borders? And most importantly, how do we secure the vital support of global investors to fuel our ambitious growth?

Through careful analysis and strategic planning, we'll navigate these challenges and pave the path for your product's global success story.

1 – Globalize Your Growth

From the moment you begin crafting your digital product, envision its global reach. It is a must.

Building a company capable of selling worldwide isn't just a bonus, it's essential for long-term success.

Here's why: global expansion unlocks exponential growth. By opening your product to users worldwide, you tap into a vast customer base, stretching across diverse markets and demographics. This translates to increased revenue and unparalleled scalability.

Embracing globalization also fuels innovation and competition. By exposing your product to a broad spectrum of needs and preferences, you're constantly challenged to adapt and improve.

This drives the development of new features, functionality, and localization options, ensuring your product resonates with specific markets.

Additionally, global competition pushes businesses to elevate their game, ultimately resulting in higher quality offerings and enhanced user experiences.

In short, going global empowers your digital product. It unlocks a vast customer base, fuels innovation, and sets the stage for sustained growth and success.

But why do only 5% of successful local companies venture into the international market?

- Lack of knowledge: Many entrepreneurs simply don't know where to start.
- Unprepared website: Websites often lack the necessary features and functionality for international business.
- Limited marketing expertise: Reaching a global audience requires specific marketing strategies.
- Shipping challenges: International shipping can be complex and costly.

These hurdles seem daunting, but they can be overcome. This blog post will equip you with the knowledge and tools you need to navigate the global market with confidence, removing barriers and realizing the full potential of your digital product.

For many entrepreneurs, the dream of selling products internationally is met with the daunting question: Where do I begin? This guide will equip you with the tools and knowledge to navigate the exciting world of global expansion.

Key Steps:

1. Market Research: Before setting sail, understand the global demand for your products. Research potential markets, considering your unique selling points and local preferences. Leverage online resources, social media, or even a trusted friend abroad to gather insights.
2. Market Selection: Start small! Dominating the world stage isn't your initial goal. Choose a single international market or cluster with high product demand. This focused approach allows for easier entry and adaptation.
3. Navigating Regulations: Familiarize yourself with the export rules and regulations of your chosen market. Understand customs, shipping protocols, and potential obstacles. Anticipate hurdles and devise solutions for smooth operation.
4. Your website/app becomes your international ambassador. Ensure it's ready for a global audience by addressing these key areas: Language Barriers: Conquer the language barrier by translating your website into relevant languages. Tools like Shiprocket 360 can effortlessly translate your content into over 90 languages, reaching a wider audience.
5. Currency Navigation: Streamline transactions by offering product prices in various currencies. Shiprocket 360's dynamic features like Currency

Updater and Dropdown Menu make this process seamless for your international customers.
6. Seamless Payment Options: Make payment a breeze for your global buyers. Integrate popular international payment gateways like PayPal and Stripe to ensure a smooth and secure checkout experience.
7. Shipping Solutions: Establish a reliable shipping system for international deliveries. Consider factors like shipping processes, competitive rates, and reliable service providers. Partnering with logistics experts like Shiprocket simplifies and optimizes your international shipping operations.
8. Once your website is ready, it's time to reach the world: Leverage SEO: Employ search engine optimization (SEO) strategies to make your products easily discoverable by international audiences. Use relevant keywords and implement local SEO tactics to ensure your products rank high in regional searches.
9. Embrace Social Media and Advertising: Utilize the power of social media platforms like Facebook, Instagram, and Twitter to connect with your target audience internationally. Consider paid advertising to further boost your visibility.
10. Tap into Marketplaces: Expand your reach through established international marketplaces like Amazon, eBay, and Etsy. These platforms offer instant access to a global customer base and simplify international selling processes.

Selling your products worldwide can be a transformative journey. By following this roadmap - conducting thorough research, focusing on a strategic market, understanding regulations, optimizing your website, and implementing effective marketing strategies - you can navigate the global marketplace with confidence and achieve remarkable success.

Meticulous planning and continuous adaptation are key to unlocking the vast potential of international growth.

Thought-Provoking Questions:

1. What are the unmet needs and frustrations of our target audience in different regions?
2. How can we adapt our product features and messaging to resonate with diverse cultural contexts?
3. What legal and regulatory hurdles need to be overcome for entering new markets?
4. How can we build trust and brand loyalty among international customers without a physical presence?
5. How can we optimize our marketing and advertising strategies for different languages and cultural nuances?
6. What are the best channels and partners for reaching our target audience in each region?
7. How can we leverage technology and data to personalize the customer experience across borders?
8. How can we build a global team with the necessary cultural awareness and market expertise?
9. How can we measure and track our global growth effectively to ensure our efforts are yielding results?
10. How can we ensure our global expansion efforts are aligned with our company's overall mission and values?

2 – How to Choose the Right Country for International Expansion

As your business thrives domestically, the lure of international expansion beckons. But which country?

But navigating the global landscape can be daunting, with 196 countries vying for your attention.

Before diving headfirst, consider these key points:

Key Steps:

1. Introspection: Are you ready for the mental and time commitment of opening in a new country? It's akin to managing a separate entity.
2. Market Fit: Analyze if your product resonates with other cultures. Trial and error, similar to testing marketing channels, can reveal hidden gems.
3. Market Research: Just as you researched your original idea, delve into potential markets. Remember, each country is a unique ecosystem that may not embrace your product as readily.
4. Cultural Proximity: While choosing a culturally familiar country seems intuitive, it may not always be the optimal choice.

5. Competitive Landscape: Understand how similar products have fared, the level of competition, and price points within your target market.
6. Advertising Costs: Higher advertising costs necessitate price adjustments to ensure profitability.
7. Workforce Needs: Consider outsourcing your workforce needs to local professionals or experimenting with freelance solutions.
8. Economic Landscape: Compare the target country's economic situation and purchasing power to your existing market. Tools like Numbeo can be helpful.
9. Regulatory Environment: Regulations may vary significantly, impacting your product launch and tax implications.
10. Marketing Channels: Research the effectiveness of your current marketing channels in the target country. Infrastructure and audience demographics may require adaptation.

Thought-Provoking Questions:

1. Is there a genuine need and demand for your product or service in the target country?
2. What are the existing alternatives available to consumers in the target market?
3. How receptive is the target market to foreign brands and products?
4. What are the cultural nuances and preferences that may affect your product's success?
5. How will your product or service be adapted to meet the specific needs of the target market?

6. How stable and predictable is the political and economic climate in the target country?
7. What are the legal and regulatory frameworks governing your industry in the target country?
8. What are the tax implications of operating in the target country?
9. What is the level of infrastructure development and access to resources in the target country?
10. What is the availability and quality of skilled workforce in the target country?

Choosing the right country is a crucial decision. If you consider these factors, you can make an informed entry into the global market and set your business on a path to sustainable success.

> *"Evolution is a process of constant branching and expansion."*
>
> *— Stephen Jay Gould*

3 – Subscription Power: Growth & Recurring Profits

The subscription model offers a compelling proposition: consistent revenue without the constant need for customer acquisition.

Its success hinges on one crucial element: delivering enduring value that continuously satisfies customers.

Strong and enduring customer relationships are the bedrock of the subscription model. Dissatisfaction or a gradual fade in perceived value are the primary triggers for cancellations.

This is where buyer personas become invaluable. Precisely understanding your customer base allows you to tailor your offerings and align them with evolving expectations.

Delivering a positive experience is essential, but it's only one piece of the puzzle. Reliable data on feature preferences and willingness to pay is crucial for crafting an optimal pricing strategy.

The deeper your understanding of your customers, the more effective your pricing will be.

In today's world, renting is increasingly the preferred option over owning. From expensive items to everyday goods, installment plans allow us to access desired products without upfront burdens, and the flexibility to walk away when the need fades.

The subscription model capitalizes on this shift in mindset, offering convenient access and the freedom to cancel, while securing predictable revenue for businesses.

Key Steps:

Step 1 - Predictability:
The subscription model's fundamental strength lies in its ability to generate stable, predictable revenue. By understanding key metrics like subscriber base, churn rate, customer acquisition, and average revenue per user (ARPU), businesses can paint a clear and consistent financial picture over time.

This clarity is highly attractive to investors, who value stability and the ability to forecast future performance.

Step 2 - Frictionless Beginnings:
The equation is straightforward: more subscriptions, more revenue. Therefore, making the subscription process effortless is paramount.

By crafting a seamless and positive customer experience, businesses can significantly increase conversion rates and onboard new subscribers with ease.

Step 3 - Automate Sales:
Encouraging customers to make multiple purchases is a crucial strategy for boosting revenue. The subscription

model serves as an automation tool for this purpose. Once a customer subscribes, subsequent purchases are made automatically in the following periods, whether monthly, weekly, or yearly.

This eliminates the need for reminders, struggles, or additional expenses to drive repeated sales.

Step 4: Customer Lifetime:
The central concern in the subscription model lies in the customer's subscription duration, often referred to as the "*average life expectancy*".

This metric fundamentally alters the dynamics, influencing how long subscribers stay committed and, consequently, how frequently they undergo automatic charges.

Hence, it becomes imperative to extend the lifetime of your customers as much as possible. Creating compelling reasons and perpetual satisfaction is key to ensuring their prolonged engagement and subscription.

Step 5: Choosing the Right Subscription Model
The subscription model encompasses various types, each tailored to suit different products.

Selecting the most fitting model for your offering is crucial. Here's an exploration of distinct subscription models and their applications:

- Confidential Information Model:
    - Experts share exclusive methods, tactics, and experiences accessible only to subscribers.
    - Example: A platform featuring detailed videos of magicians demonstrating exclusive tricks.
- Box on Door Model:
    - Subscribers receive a physical or digital product automatically at chosen intervals, adding an element of surprise.
    - Example: Monthly delivery of a mystery box containing items like a book, toy, snack, or daily meal.
- All for One Price Model:
    - Ideal for frequent consumption, customers pay a fixed fee for unlimited access to a diverse range of physical or digital products.
    - Example: Successful implementation by platforms like Spotify and Netflix.
- Apprentice Model:
    - A guided, one-on-one process aimed at development, change, and specialization in a specific subject.
    - Example: Services provided by professionals like psychologists, fitness instructors, and life coaches.
- As Many Models as You Want:
    - Allows customers to use a product or service for a specific period, avoiding the need for a full purchase.
    - Example: Utilized by platforms like Airbnb and car rental services.
- Wingman Model:
    - Complementary products are sold cheaply, and customers are then subscribed to high-margin accessories or necessities.

- Example: Nespresso sells coffee machines at a low cost and offers subscription-based coffee capsules for ongoing revenue.
- Dating Model:
    - Offers a free or low-cost trial period, allowing users to experience the product before committing to a subscription.
    - Example: Many applications on the Apple App Store follow this model.
- Premium Model:
    - Provides free content to a target audience but reserves premium content exclusively for subscribers.
    - Example: YouTube's "Join" feature.
- Special Club Model:
    - Offers exclusive subscriptions to high-value customers, providing additional services, priorities, or special events.
    - Example: Soho Houses catering to individuals with high income levels and significant purchasing volumes.
- Staircase Model:
    - Tailors subscription packages with varying features and prices to meet the diverse needs of a customer base.
    - Example: Netflix offers different-priced subscriptions with varying features, such as standard and ultra HD options.

Choosing the right subscription model requires a thoughtful consideration of your product, target audience, and business goals.

Each model brings its unique advantages, and finding the perfect fit is key to maximizing both customer satisfaction and revenue.

Step 6 - Optimizing Subscription Packages:
In your subscription models, adjusting the content, price, and duration of the packages is a straightforward process.

This flexibility allows you to experiment, testing different combinations to discern which package resonates most effectively with your audience.

Furthermore, you can meticulously measure the performance of each variant, gaining valuable insights into the preferences and behaviors of your customers.

This iterative approach empowers you to refine and tailor your subscription offerings, ensuring they align seamlessly with your business goals and the evolving needs of your clientele.

Step 7 - Analyzing Package Performance:
A crucial aspect to bear in mind is never to directly compare the performance of new packages solely based on acceptance rates.

For instance, when presenting both a 9.99 TL/Month and a 99.99 TL/Year package, the acceptance rate for the annual package–indicating the ratio of unique viewers of the payment page to those initiating the annual package– might be lower than the monthly option.

However, it's essential to recognize that, despite the lower acceptance rate, the annual package yields a substantial upfront payment of 99.99 TL.

This strategic perspective ensures a comprehensive understanding of the financial impact and long-term benefits associated with different subscription offerings.

Step 8 - Maximizing LTV:
Conversely, if subscribers opting for the monthly package exhibit an average retention of 10 months or more, acquiring monthly subscribers becomes a lucrative source of income.

To identify the optimal package, it is essential to analyze this scenario in conjunction with the overall income potential over the average customer lifespan (LTV = Life Time Value) and the acceptance rate.

This comprehensive evaluation allows for a strategic approach to selecting subscription packages, ensuring not only sustained income but also aligning with the preferences and behaviors of your customer base.

Step 9 - Cash Flow Challenges:
One notable drawback of subscription models lies in the potential for a significant negative impact on cash flow during the initial stages of product launch.

However, there is no cause for concern if you possess a confident understanding of the Life Time Value (LTV). In such cases, it is advisable to persist in strategic spending. In instances where the LTV is uncertain, a prudent approach involves aligning acquisition costs with day-one revenue–the income derived from charging the subscription price once.

This precautionary measure safeguards against the worst-case scenario, offering a buffer against potential cash flow challenges.

Step 10 - Tailoring for Audiences:

Tailor distinct subscription packages, pricing structures, and content offerings based on geographical location, language preferences, and demographic profiles.

This strategic customization empowers you to extract the highest possible revenue from the diverse audiences you engage with.

By aligning your subscription approach with the unique characteristics of each market segment, you not only enhance customer satisfaction but also optimize your income potential across varied audiences.

Thought-Provoking Questions:

1. How does the subscription business model align with the unique value proposition of your product or service, and how can you enhance this alignment for increased customer appeal?
2. In what ways can you leverage data analytics to understand customer behaviors, preferences, and churn patterns, ultimately refining your subscription offerings?

3. How do you balance the need for competitive pricing to attract subscribers with the imperative of maximizing revenue to ensure a sustainable business model?
4. What innovative approaches can be employed to continually add value to your subscription packages, fostering long-term customer loyalty and reducing churn rates?
5. Considering the dynamic nature of consumer preferences, how do you stay agile and adapt your subscription models to emerging trends in the mobile app market?
6. What strategies can be implemented to effectively communicate the value proposition of your subscription packages, ensuring potential subscribers understand the benefits they stand to gain?
7. How can you strategically diversify your subscription offerings across different markets, considering variations in cultural preferences, economic factors, and consumer behaviors?
8. What role does customer feedback play in shaping and refining your subscription models, and how can you actively encourage and utilize this feedback for continuous improvement?
9. In terms of customer acquisition costs, what measures can be implemented to optimize spending while ensuring a positive return on investment for each acquired subscriber?
10. How do you approach the scalability of your subscription business model, especially as your user base grows, and what infrastructure and systems are in place to support this growth effectively?

4 – Make a Mobile App

Developing a mobile app with a solid business model is a savvy way to launch a global company.

But have you ever wondered how those ubiquitous apps you use daily became so popular?

Often, we think, "I wish there was an app for that!" But not every app idea will succeed, and popularity alone isn't enough. To build a sustainable, profitable mobile app business, you need a rock-solid commercial model.

Let's shift our focus from free app popularity to building a lasting, revenue-generating company. Think of your app as a customer access channel, similar to a website or store. Why is this channel so opportune?

A large portion of users in app stores have pre-registered credit cards, making purchases a one-click process. This represents the biggest opportunity.

Research shows that the more steps involved in purchasing, the higher the abandonment rate. A staggering 67.91% of users globally abandon their purchases before completion.

Think about it: 68 out of 100 people who express initial interest give up before even reaching for their wallets. This happens because we often make impulsive buying decisions.

Mobile app stores capitalize on this by offering pre-defined credit cards and one-click purchases.

The convenience of pre-defined cards led to the development of Masterpass and similar quick payment systems on websites and other channels.

The shorter and simpler the purchasing process, the higher your sales and revenue. Amazon Go exemplifies this perfectly.

Imagine a convenience store with no cashiers or attendants. You enter by scanning your phone, grab what you want, and walk out, hands-free. It sounds like science fiction, but Amazon made it a reality thanks to technology.

Here's how it works:

- You have the Amazon app, linked to your pre-defined credit card and Amazon account.
- Scanning a QR code at the entrance registers your card. From then on, you are essentially a credit card.
- The smart basket you carry uses NFC technology to detect your purchases.
- As you leave, the basket communicates the total amount to the exit door, which charges your card.

Why did Amazon go to such lengths? To eliminate the entire purchasing process, removing any hesitation or thought about price, alternatives, etc.

They want you to buy purely based on the ease of the experience.

Optimizing your mobile app's buying experience is paramount. The goal is to drive users towards the "buy" button with such ease and confidence that your business flourishes.

Building a thriving mobile app business requires more than just a captivating idea. It demands a seamless, user-friendly experience that motivates purchases and generates sustained revenue.

Key Steps:

Step 1: Finding a Profitable Idea

To unearth a revenue-generating mobile app idea, or assess the viability of your existing concept, start with the Idea Development section (see Idea).

Step 2: Choosing Your Business Model

After identifying your app idea, select the business model that aligns with your monetization goals. Here's a breakdown of the most common models used by mobile app companies:

1. In-app Ads:
    - Popularity: Widely used due to its ease of implementation.
    - Challenges: Low survival rate for apps solely reliant on ads (less than 1%). Requires high active user

base to generate significant revenue. Users often find ads disruptive.
- Getting Started: Integrate SDKs from Google AdMob, Facebook Audience Network, Unity.ads, etc.
- Maximizing Revenue: Implement Ad Mediation to connect to multiple ad networks simultaneously and display ads with the highest bids. Consider Admost for this purpose.

2. Paid Application:
   - Simplistic: Users pay a one-time fee to download the app.
   - Challenges: Most users prefer free apps, leading them to seek alternatives. In-app purchases generally outperform paid downloads.

3. In-app Purchases:
   - Flexible: Users download the app for free and access basic features. Additional features require payment.
   - Performance: Works best in mobile games, where virtual currencies and game dynamics are prevalent.
   - Popular Example: "Remove ads" functionality offers users ad-free experience for a fee.

4. In-app Subscription:
   - Sustainable: Considered one of the best models (see Focus on Subscription).
   - Concept: User downloads the app for free and uses basic features. Premium features are behind a "subscription wall."
   - Subscription Model: User pays recurring fees (weekly, monthly, yearly) to access premium features.

- Payment Convenience: Charges are automatically deducted from the credit card registered in the app store.
- Subscription Management: App stores automatically update payment information or retry failed payments for a period (60 days on average).

5. Commission (Offer Wall):
    - Rewarding Videos: Users earn in-app rewards for watching advertising videos. App owners receive $1-$5 per 1000 video views from advertisers.
    - CPA (Cost Per Action): Users take specific actions (subscribe, become a member, fill out a form, download an app) through links within your app, earning app owners a commission from the advertised company.

Step 3: Mastering the Art of Mobile App Marketing

Identifying the optimal marketing channel for your mobile app is crucial. While Google Ads and Facebook Ads are popular choices, let's unveil a powerful hidden gem: Apple Search Ads.

Unlocking the Power of Apple Search Ads:

- Exclusively for iOS Apps: Developed by Apple specifically for the App Store, this platform is a must-try for any iOS app developer seeking global reach.
- Top Billing for Your App: In simple terms, for a fee (CPT or cost per tap), Search Ads ensures your app appears at the top of search results for targeted

keywords. Think of it as the App Store's answer to Google Search Ads.
- Reaching Your Ideal Audience: Imagine a user seeking "photo editing" or "Instagram" in the App Store. This is your target audience, actively searching for apps like yours. Search Ads positions your app at the forefront of their search, maximizing visibility.
- Engagement That Matters: Unlike other channels where you interrupt users with irrelevant ads, here, the user is actively seeking apps like yours. This translates to higher engagement and a 4-5 times greater conversion rate compared to traditional channels (based on experience).
- Acquiring High-Value Customers: Not only does Search Ads attract users, but it attracts users who convert into paying customers. You gain customers who make purchases, not just downloads, at a significantly lower cost (approximately one-fifth, based on experience).
- A Boon for Organic Growth: Beyond targeted acquisition, Search Ads also boosts your organic downloads by 8-10 times. This "ASO (App Store Optimization) effect" is achieved as your app gains traction through paid advertising, signaling to Apple that users love your app. This, in turn, leads to higher organic ranking in categories and other lists.
- Global Reach: Promote your app across 60+ countries. While not yet available in every App Store, you can advertise in accessible countries from any location.

While Search Ads offers incredible benefits, it's worth noting that the ranking algorithm considers over 15-20 factors.

However, the key takeaway is that apps leveraging Search Ads consistently experience significant ranking jumps, leading to increased organic app visibility and downloads.

By mastering this powerful tool, you can unlock a world of opportunities and achieve global success for your mobile app.

Step 4: ASO: Optimizing Your App for Success

In the competitive world of mobile apps, App Store Optimization (ASO) is your key to unlocking discoverability and downloads.

ASO involves perfecting the information, data, and images displayed within app stores like Apple's App Store and Google Play.

Why is ASO crucial? App stores categorize apps by function, displaying similar apps together in lists. Here's the catch: over 80% of users never look beyond the third page of these lists, and a staggering 99% don't venture past the tenth. This means your app essentially becomes invisible if it doesn't rank within the top 10.

Consider this: there are millions of mobile apps available, yet only 1% achieve true success. Users typically have only 30-40 apps on their phones, actively using only 3-5 daily. While the market offers immense potential, a near-perfect idea and exceptional marketing skills are essential for breaking through the noise.

ASO is the cornerstone of effective mobile app marketing. Both Apple and Android utilize hidden algorithms to rank apps, but experienced developers have identified the key criteria these algorithms prioritize. These are the areas you should focus on:

1. Descriptive App Names: Ditch the "sexy" names and opt for clarity. Users search for apps to solve problems and make their lives easier. If the app name accurately reflects its function, users are more likely to download it. Imagine searching for "accounting software" and finding an app named "Excalibur." Would you download it? Probably not. Instead, "Easy Accounting" or "Quick Accounts" would be more appealing and relevant to your search.

2. Meeting User Expectations: Don't mislead potential users with fancy names. Ensure your app name clearly describes its purpose and functionality. By aligning your app name with what it does, you increase its chances of being discovered and downloaded.

3. Keywords: One of the most crucial aspects of App Store Optimization (ASO) is maximizing your keyword usage.

App stores register your app's functionalities based on your chosen keywords during installation. These keywords determine whether your app appears relevant to user searches, making your allotted space incredibly valuable.

However, brute force keyword stuffing won't suffice. Established apps, likely your competitors, have likely claimed the most popular keywords for years. Competing with them for top rankings directly is a near-impossible uphill battle for a new app.

Instead, focus on smart keyword selection. Utilize services like Mobile Action, AppAnnie, or Sensor Tower to identify less competitive, but relevant keywords. This allows you to fill your keyword space with strategic terms, increasing your app's discoverability.

Here are some key strategies for maximizing your keyword space:

- Don't waste space with commas: Omit spaces after commas, allowing you to insert 2-3 additional keywords. App stores recognize individual words even without spaces.
- Avoid redundant terms: Don't list variations of the same word or pluralize words ("photo editor", "photo", "editor" should be "photo,editor"). App stores combine similar keywords, so repetition is unnecessary.
- Leverage existing keywords: The app name and subtitle are already considered keywords by app stores, so there's no need to repeat them. Think of it as a hierarchy: strongest keywords in the name, followed by the subtitle, and finally, additional keywords. This underscores the importance of choosing a descriptive app name.

Smart keyword strategies unlock app discoverability, attracting more users and giving you a competitive edge in the mobile market. Success goes beyond brute force. It's about strategically selecting and efficiently utilizing your limited keyword space.

4. Visuals that Captivate at First Glance

Three key visuals define your app in app stores: icons, screenshots, and app usage videos.

While the first two are mandatory, consider adding a video for an edge. Videos are still underutilized, giving you a head start if you have one.

Ranking high is crucial. If your visual language doesn't stand out from competitors, you'll easily be overlooked.

Analyze your target list: study their icons, screenshots, and video usage. Aim for equal or better execution initially, then strive to be dramatically different and better in the next stage.

Text on screenshots matters, too. Persuasive descriptions are essential. Keep it short and to the point. Mobile screens demand large fonts, easily readable at a glance. Opt for short, impactful phrases instead of elaborate sentences.

Use trust-building elements like "Ranked #1 in 30 countries," "Recommended by X Magazine," "1 Million Happy Users," etc., to reassure potential users.

5. Short and Sweet Descriptions

Long, descriptive texts are a turn-off. Keep it brief, clear, and simple. List all features in bullet points for easy navigation.

6. Category Choice Matters

Choose the category your app truly belongs to. Don't be tempted by crowded or competitive categories just because of their size. Users browsing there aren't expecting your app.

7. Harness the Power of Positive Reviews

Positive reviews are a major ranking factor. Higher ratings translate to higher rankings. Encourage satisfied users to leave positive comments within the app. But be strategic! Don't prompt unhappy users - it can backfire. Offer rating prompts only when you know the user is happy.

Consider Instagram's approach:

- A prompt when users first install the app.
- A prompt when their post receives a significant number of likes.

Which scenario would be more likely to result in a 5-star rating?

Step 5: Choosing the Right Platform for Profit

With 87% of the world using Android, it might seem like the obvious choice for your first app release.

However, in a revenue-focused business, targeting the audience more likely to convert is key. While only 13% use iOS, it accounts for a staggering 65.4% of the mobile app market's total revenue.

This translates to an astonishing 12.5 times greater purchase propensity among iOS users compared to Android.

Additionally, serving a smaller iOS user base can result in higher revenue per customer, making it a more attractive option from a customer relationship perspective.

This doesn't mean neglecting Android entirely. Targeting high-power Android users, like those with top-model Samsung phones, can still yield significant income, especially when focused marketing efforts are employed.

If development ease is a priority, Google's Flutter platform allows you to build apps for both iOS, Android, and web using a single code base, offering a more efficient approach.

Step 6: Choosing the Right Country

Targeting countries with high mobile app revenue per capita and a sizable population is ideal.

My research consistently points to two key markets: America and Japan.

These two countries boast a significantly higher iOS usage rate compared to the global average: 58.6% in America and 64.3% in Japan, translating to 4-5 times the global average.

This explains their consistent presence as top revenue-generating markets.

While other English-speaking countries and China might occasionally offer promising results, for sustained high income, conquering America and Japan is your best bet, based on my experience.

Choosing the right platform and target audience can significantly impact your app's success. You can make strategic decisions that pave the way for a thriving mobile app business with prioritizing revenue and considering user behavior.

Thought-Provoking Questions:

1. How will you disrupt existing industries or create entirely new ones? Can your app's impact extend beyond its immediate function and spark broader change in the world?
2. Can your app address global challenges and contribute to social good? Can you leverage technology to solve critical social or environmental issues and positively impact the lives of millions?
3. How will your app's success empower marginalized communities or promote equality? Can you actively

address inequalities and create a more inclusive and equitable digital landscape?
4. How will you leverage the power of artificial intelligence and machine learning to personalize user experiences and enhance functionalities? Can you create an app that adapts to individual user needs and preferences, offering a truly unique and valuable experience?
5. Can your app be integrated into emerging technologies like the metaverse or Web3, opening up new possibilities for user interaction and engagement? Are you exploring ways to leverage the potential of these nascent technologies to create a truly cutting-edge app experience?
6. How will you cultivate a thriving developer community around your app, fostering innovation and collaboration? Can you create an ecosystem that attracts talented developers and encourages them to contribute to the growth and evolution of your app?
7. How will you create a culture of ethical and responsible development, ensuring your app is used for good and not harm? Are you committed to developing your app with transparency, accountability, and a strong focus on user safety and well-being?
8. How will you inspire and empower users to become creators and contributors, rather than mere consumers? Can your app be a platform for self-expression, creativity, and collaboration, fostering a vibrant and engaged community?
9. How will your app transcend the limitations of smartphones and integrate seamlessly into the broader digital ecosystem? Can you create an app that interacts

with other devices, platforms, and services, offering a truly interconnected and convenient experience?
10. What is the legacy you want your app to leave on the world? What impact do you hope your app will have on individuals, communities, and society as a whole?

These questions are not meant to have simple answers. They are designed to push your thinking beyond the immediate and encourage you to explore the full potential of your app idea.

Wrestling with these profound inquiries can be the catalyst to crafting a mobile app that transcends mere financial gain and leaves a lasting, positive mark on the world.

> *"Mobile is becoming not only the new digital hub but also the bridge to the physical world. That's why mobile will affect more than just your digital operations - it will transform your entire business."*
>
> *— Thomas Husson*

5 – Make a Mobile Game

Building a mobile game offers a unique opportunity to tap into a vast audience and create a lasting impact.

With their accessibility and diverse player base, mobile games have become a powerful platform for entertainment, offering the potential for financial gain, business growth, and even social connection.

Developers have the chance to bring joy and excitement to millions, shaping experiences and fostering communities through the magic of interactive storytelling and engaging gameplay.

Beyond entertainment, mobile games can also be educational, promoting learning and cognitive development, while fostering creativity and problem-solving skills.

These reasons combined make building a mobile game a significant undertaking, one with the potential to touch countless lives and leave a lasting legacy on the world of entertainment and beyond.

Türkiye holds a unique position in the world of mobile gaming. This vibrant nation boasts a thriving ecosystem of game developers, responsible for some of the most iconic and beloved mobile games of our time.

From Peak Games and Masomo to Gram Games, the creators of Angry Birds, Candy Crush, Clash of Clans, and the viral phenomenon Flappy Bird, Türkiye has consistently produced mobile gaming giants.

These are just a few examples of the countless success stories that have cemented Türkiye's position as a global leader in mobile gaming.

A recent study by the Global Mobile Gaming Confederation (GMGC) forecasts a staggering $12 billion market by 2026, driven by a phenomenal annual growth rate of 209%. This explosive growth signifies the enormous potential mobile gaming holds for businesses venturing into this exciting realm.

Several factors contribute to the phenomenal success of mobile gaming. Firstly, its reach is unparalleled. The ubiquity of mobile devices grants access to people of all ages and backgrounds, creating a vast and diverse audience. This offers game developers a sprawling canvas to unleash their creativity and bring their vision to life.

Secondly, mobile games are renowned for their accessibility. Players can instantly jump into the action during a mundane train ride or a short break, making them ideal for busy schedules. This ease of access lowers the barrier to entry and allows more people to join the global gaming community.

Beyond entertainment and financial gain, mobile game development holds a deeper significance. It empowers creators to bring joy and excitement to millions. With every game, developers have the potential to transport players to fantastical worlds, ignite imaginations, and forge lasting connections.

The power to evoke smiles and laughter through a mobile game is a truly remarkable gift, making game developers more than just creators, but ambassadors of joy and wonder.

As Türkiye continues to be at the forefront of the mobile gaming revolution, its influence on the global landscape is undeniable. With its talented developers, passionate community, and unwavering commitment to innovation, Türkiye is poised to drive the mobile gaming industry to even greater heights, leaving a lasting mark on the world of entertainment for generations to come.

Key Steps:

1. In-Depth Market Research:
Begin by thoroughly understanding the mobile gaming market. Identify trends, player preferences, and potential gaps to create a game that stands out.

2. Define Unique Value Proposition:
Clearly articulate what sets your game apart. Whether it's innovative gameplay mechanics, a captivating story, or stunning visuals, a unique selling point is essential.

3. User-Centric Design:
Prioritize user experience (UX) and user interface (UI) design. Intuitive controls, appealing visuals, and seamless navigation contribute to player satisfaction.

4. Scalable Development Architecture:
Build a robust and scalable architecture to accommodate future updates and expansions. Consider the potential for in-app purchases and multiplayer features.

5. Engaging Gameplay Mechanics:
Craft gameplay that is not only entertaining but also keeps players coming back. Incorporate elements like challenges, rewards, and social interactions to enhance engagement.

6. Thorough Testing:
Conduct extensive testing to identify and address bugs, glitches, and other issues. Test the game with a diverse group of users to ensure a broad perspective on its performance.

7. Monetization Strategy:
Develop a well-thought-out monetization strategy. This could involve in-app purchases, ads, or a combination of both. Balance the need for revenue with providing value to players.

8. Strategic Marketing and Launch:
Create a pre-launch marketing strategy to build anticipation. Leverage social media, influencers, and other channels. Ensure a polished launch with effective app store optimization.

9. Community Building:
Foster a community around your game. Encourage player interactions, gather feedback, and implement updates based on community suggestions. A loyal player base is crucial for long-term success.

10. Data-Driven Iteration:
Utilize analytics to track player behavior, retention rates, and other key metrics. Regularly update the game based on this data to enhance player experience and keep the content fresh.

Strategic framework for game design that encompasses both creativity and practicality.

1. Conceptual Clarity:
Begin with a clear and concise concept for your game. Define its core theme, narrative, and overall purpose. The more focused and unique your concept, the more likely it is to resonate with players.

2. Player-Centric Approach:
Understand your target audience deeply. Consider their preferences, playstyles, and expectations. Design the game to be enjoyable and accessible, catering to the needs and desires of your players.

3. Iterative Prototyping:
Develop prototypes early and iterate on them regularly. This allows you to test mechanics, gather feedback, and refine your game's design before investing significant resources.

4. Engaging Gameplay Loops:
Craft compelling and rewarding gameplay loops. Ensure that players are consistently motivated to progress, providing a sense of accomplishment and maintaining their interest over time.

5. Balancing Act:
Achieve a delicate balance between challenge and accessibility. A well-balanced game keeps players engaged without becoming frustrating. Gradually introduce complexity to maintain a sense of progression.

6. Story Integration:
If your game involves a narrative, seamlessly integrate it into the gameplay. Ensure that the story enhances the player's experience rather than feeling like a separate element.

7. Visual Cohesion:
Establish a cohesive and visually appealing art style. Consistent aesthetics contribute to a memorable and immersive gaming experience. Align the visuals with the game's theme and mood.

8. Dynamic Sound Design:
Invest in dynamic and immersive sound design. Audio cues, music, and effects enhance the atmosphere and contribute significantly to the overall feel of the game.

9. User-Generated Content (UGC):
If applicable, incorporate features that allow players to create and share content. UGC not only extends the life of

your game but also fosters a sense of community among players.

10. Post-Launch Support:
Plan for post-launch support and updates. Regularly analyze player feedback, address issues promptly, and introduce new content to keep the game fresh and maintain player engagement.

To find the perfect game mechanics:

1. Define Core Objectives:
Clearly outline the primary objectives and goals of your game. Whether it's competition, collaboration, exploration, or storytelling, having a clear focus will guide your choice of mechanics.

2. Player Engagement Analysis:
Analyze your target audience and understand what engages them. For instance, if your audience enjoys strategic thinking, consider turn-based mechanics like those in chess or Civilization.

3. Iterative Prototyping:
Prototype various mechanics to test their impact on player engagement. Minecraft, for example, evolved through multiple prototypes, eventually settling on its innovative sandbox gameplay.

4. Player Agency:
Introduce mechanics that provide players with a sense of agency and control over the game world. The branching narrative in games like "Life is Strange" is an excellent

example, allowing players to shape the story based on their choices.

5. Balancing Challenge and Skill:
Design mechanics that strike a balance between challenge and the player's skill level. Dark Souls is renowned for its challenging combat mechanics, rewarding players who master the intricacies of the system.

6. Unique Selling Point (USP):
Identify and highlight a unique selling point in your mechanics. Portal's use of the portal gun, enabling players to manipulate space, is a prime example of a distinctive game mechanic.

7. Accessibility and Depth:
Ensure mechanics are accessible to new players while providing depth for experienced ones. Rocket League's simple premise of soccer with rocket-powered cars is easy to grasp but allows for advanced skills and strategies.

8. Player Feedback Systems:
Implement feedback systems to keep players informed about their actions and their impact on the game. The "bullet time" mechanic in Max Payne, slowing down time during intense gunfights, provides immediate feedback on successful actions.

9. Emotional Impact:
Consider the emotional impact of your mechanics. The time-traveling mechanic in "Braid" not only challenges players intellectually but also evokes emotional responses as the narrative unfolds.

10. Player-Created Emergent Gameplay:
Encourage emergent gameplay by allowing players to create unexpected scenarios through your mechanics. The open-world nature of "The Legend of Zelda: Breath of the Wild" fosters countless player-driven experiences.

To help you kickstart, here's a list of various game mechanics along with brief descriptions:

- Role-Playing Game (RPG) Mechanics:
    - Players assume the roles of characters in a fictional world, progressing through a narrative, gaining experience, and improving their abilities. Example: "The Elder Scrolls V: Skyrim."
- First-Person Shooter (FPS) Mechanics:
    - Players experience the game through the eyes of the character, engaging in combat with a focus on precision and aiming. Example: "Call of Duty" series.
- Platformer Mechanics:
    - Games characterized by jumping between platforms to navigate environments. Example: "Super Mario Bros."
- Strategy Mechanics:
    - Players plan and execute strategies to achieve goals, often involving resource management and decision-making. Example: "Civilization VI."
- Simulation Mechanics:
    - Games that simulate real-world activities or systems. Examples include "The Sims" for life simulation and "SimCity" for city building.
- Puzzle Mechanics:

- Challenges that require problem-solving skills, logic, and pattern recognition. Example: "Tetris."
- Stealth Mechanics:
  - Players avoid detection and navigate environments covertly. Example: "Metal Gear Solid" series.
- Survival Mechanics:
  - Players must manage resources, avoid threats, and survive in challenging environments. Example: "Don't Starve."
- Open-World Mechanics:
  - Expansive game worlds that allow players to explore freely, often with a non-linear narrative. Example: "The Legend of Zelda: Breath of the Wild."
- Time-Manipulation Mechanics:
  - Games where players can control or manipulate time, impacting gameplay and puzzles. Example: "Braid."
- Roguelike Mechanics:
  - Games featuring procedurally generated levels, permadeath, and often randomized items. Example: "FTL: Faster Than Light."
- Augmented Reality (AR) Mechanics:
  - Games that overlay digital elements onto the real world through a device like a smartphone. Example: "Pokémon GO."
- Real-Time Strategy (RTS) Mechanics:
  - Players make strategic decisions in real-time, managing resources and commanding units. Example: "StarCraft."
- Point-and-Click Adventure Mechanics:

- Players interact with the game world by clicking on objects to solve puzzles and progress the story. Example: "Monkey Island."
- Battle Royale Mechanics:
    - Last-player-standing competition in a shrinking play area. Example: "Fortnite" and "PlayerUnknown's Battlegrounds (PUBG)."

Thought-Provoking Questions:

1. How does your game provide a unique and irresistible value proposition to users, setting it apart from existing mobile games?
2. What innovative and player-friendly monetization strategies can you implement to generate substantial revenue without compromising user experience?
3. How will you design the game to foster long-term player engagement, encouraging daily or frequent interaction over an extended period?
4. In what ways can you leverage social integration to enhance the game experience, promote virality, and increase user acquisition organically?
5. How will the game evolve over time, and what scalability measures are in place to accommodate a growing user base and changing market trends?
6. Are you incorporating emerging technologies, such as augmented reality (AR) or virtual reality (VR), to stay ahead of industry trends and offer a cutting-edge experience?
7. How will you utilize player data to inform game updates, enhance user experience, and make data-driven decisions for ongoing improvements?

8. What strategies will you employ to seamlessly integrate the game across multiple platforms, ensuring accessibility and a consistent experience for players?
9. How do you plan to build and nurture a dedicated community around your game, fostering player interaction and loyalty?
10. How will you tailor the game to have universal appeal, considering cultural differences and preferences to attract a global player base?

"Education should learn from the positive side of gaming - reward, accomplishment, and fun."

— Sebastian Thrun

6 – Securing Investment for Your Product

Possessing investors' contact information doesn't guarantee funding. You have to make them believe.

Whether large or small, investors primarily seek substantial returns on their invested capital over time. So, why embrace the risk?

Simply put, traditional investment instruments don't offer the potential for outsized profits.

However, in poor or economically fragile nations, the equation changes. Guaranteeing 10-20% returns through bank deposits versus investing in uncertain ventures presents no fair competition.

Risk-averse individuals naturally gravitate towards secure returns.

Therefore, the answer to "why entrepreneurship struggles in poor countries" is surprisingly straightforward.

Silicon Valley's near-zero or negative interest rates paint a contrasting picture. Negative interest means your $100 deposit becomes $99 after a year. Would you invest? Of course not.

This stark difference is why investors are readily available in San Francisco but rare in resource-constrained environments.

Starting your venture in a poor or economically weak nation is like entering a barren landscape. However, producing in such a country while selling internationally opens doors to both local and foreign investors.

The reason? Your revenue streams are in the globally coveted reserve currency, the US dollar.

Key Steps:

1. Demonstrate Market Readiness: Before seeking investment or support, convince everyone you approach that your product is ready to face the market and meet customer needs. This involves completing the steps outlined in this book.
2. Develop a Comprehensive Business Plan: Craft a 5-year plan detailing your product's revenue and expenses, estimated customer base, and sales projections.
3. Craft a Compelling Pitch: Present your business idea in a clear, concise, and compelling manner to investors. Your story is crucial, but avoid lengthy presentations. Aim for a 10-slide deck covering the following key points:
    1. Problem: Identify the problem your idea addresses and how it solves a genuine need or solves it differently.
    2. Solution: Clearly explain your proposed solution and its benefits.

3. **Business Model:** Describe how your project will generate revenue and ensure sustainable growth.
4. **Unique Selling Proposition:** Highlight the "wow" factor that sets you apart from competitors, such as technology or innovation.
5. **Marketing Strategy:** Explain how you will reach your target audience, acquire customers, and manage customer acquisition costs.
6. **Competitive Landscape:** Identify your competitors and explain your competitive advantage.
7. **Feasibility:** Demonstrate the practicality of your idea, addressing potential technological hurdles.
8. **Market Size & Predictions:** Estimate the market size, potential customer base, and user conversion rates. Project your growth trajectory compared to similar products.
9. **Development Status:** Showcase any prototypes, demos, or progress made so far. Explain any obstacles hindering development.
10. **Call to Action:** Conclude with a clear call to action, whether it's a request for a follow-up meeting, demo trial, or investment commitment.

4. **Identify Potential Investors:** Research and identify leading venture capitalists and government sponsors both in your country and internationally. Refer to the "Investment & Support Resources" section for assistance.
5. **Leverage University Support:** All major universities in your country, especially ITU and Yıldız Technical University, offer entrepreneurship support programs. Reach out to them to explore available assistance.

6. Seek Industry Support: Contact prominent figures in your industry with whom you have established relationships. They may provide valuable feedback and potentially become mentors, connecting you to wider networks.
7. Select the Right Investors: Not all investors are a good fit. Carefully research and shortlist potential investors based on the following criteria:
    - Investment History: Have they invested in businesses similar to yours?
    - Team Expertise: Do they have experience supporting entrepreneurs like you?
    - Investment Terms: What are their typical investment rates and amounts?
    - Entrepreneur Feedback: What do other entrepreneurs say about their experience working with these investors?
8. Determine Funding Needs: Investors want to know exactly how much money you need and how you plan to use it. Be prepared to justify your request, explaining why you need $1 million instead of $500,000 or $5 million.
    - Personnel Costs: Salary estimates for your team members.
    - Marketing Costs: Projected marketing and advertising expenses.
    - Technical Costs: Software, hardware, server, and licensing fees.
    - Operational Costs: Rent, utilities, and office supplies.
    - Equipment Needs: Any necessary equipment and its cost.

- Funding Timeline: The timeframe for utilizing the requested funds.
9. Manage Equity Sharing: Understand the percentage of your company you will offer investors in exchange for their funding. Be aware that holding less than a 50% share can limit your control over critical decisions. Use resources like Foundrs and Gust to calculate fair investor equity.
10. Secure Early Partners: Identify experienced individuals who believe in your vision and are willing to roll up their sleeves as partners. These early employees are invaluable investors who bring crucial expertise and commitment beyond financial support. Refer to the "Build a Team" section for further guidance.

Thought-Provoking Questions:

1. What problem are you solving that no one else is talking about?
   - Highlight a unique problem your startup addresses, sparking curiosity and demonstrating innovation.
2. How are you disrupting the existing market, and why is now the right time?
   - Explain the competitive landscape and how your solution disrupts it, emphasizing the urgency and timing of your venture.
3. What are the three most significant risks your startup faces, and how are you mitigating them?
   - Transparency and proactive risk management demonstrate a well-thought-out plan and inspire investor confidence.

4. How will you use the investment to achieve measurable milestones and demonstrate traction?
   - Show a clear roadmap for utilizing the funds and achieving key goals, quantifying progress and potential returns.
5. What are your long-term vision and exit strategy for investors?
   - Illustrate a clear vision for the company's future and a pathway for investors to realize their returns, showcasing long-term potential.
6. How will you attract and retain top talent in your competitive industry?
   - Explain your talent acquisition strategy and demonstrate your ability to build a strong, committed team.
7. What is your unfair advantage, and how will you sustain it?
   - Identify a unique advantage that sets you apart and explain how you will maintain it over competitors.
8. How are you leveraging technology to scale your business and reach a global audience?
   - Highlight your use of technology to achieve scalability and market expansion, demonstrating forward-thinking strategies.
9. What are the ethical considerations of your business model, and how will you ensure responsible growth?
   - Address potential ethical concerns and demonstrate your commitment to responsible business practices, attracting socially conscious investors.
10. How will you measure the impact of your venture beyond financial success?
    - Go beyond mere profits and articulate the positive impact your startup will create on society or the

environment, attracting investors who value social impact.

Implementing these steps and showcasing a well-developed plan, a compelling vision, and a strong team will significantly increase your chances of securing the necessary support to launch your startup successfully.

"If you come in with a theory, and a plan and no data, and you're 1 of the next 1000, it's going to be far far harder to raise money."

*— **Marc Andreessen***

7 – Mastering Your Money in the Global Market

Navigating the complexities of international business demands a firm grasp on financial management.

From currency fluctuations to budgeting, every aspect needs careful attention to ensure your company's success.

While the title of "boss" brings great satisfaction, it also comes with immense responsibility. You'll face long to-do lists, juggle multiple roles, and oversee all financial operations.

In essence, you become the company's accountant, responsible for tracking cash flow and making informed financial decisions.

Key Steps:

Step 1: Separate Personal and Business Finances
Open a dedicated business account to ensure clear financial separation and simplify accounting.

Step 2: Invest Idle Capital Wisely
Explore low-risk, high-return investment options specifically designed for businesses. Don't let your hard-earned money sit idle.

Step 3: Monitor Currency Fluctuations

As you expand internationally, closely track the currencies of your target markets and their relationship to the US dollar. Make informed decisions based on currency movements.

Step 4: Prioritize Insurance

Protect your business with comprehensive insurance coverage. This safeguards your company from unforeseen events and ensures smooth operations.

Step 5: Invest in Research and Development (R&D)

Allocate a portion of your budget to R&D, fueling innovation and driving future growth. This helps you stay competitive and adapt to market changes.

Step 6: Rent Instead of Buying Equipment

Consider renting equipment and resources instead of making large upfront purchases. This improves capital flexibility and allows you to adapt to changing needs.

Step 7: Monitor Project Timelines Closely

Delays can be costly. Closely monitor project timelines and deliverables to avoid wasted time and resources.

Step 8: Create and Stick to a Budget

Plan ahead and establish a comprehensive budget at the beginning of the year. Analyze your income and expenses regularly, making adjustments as needed.

Step 9: Seek Investors

Launching a business solely on personal funds carries significant risk. Look for investors who believe in your vision and share the entrepreneurial journey.

Step 10: Leverage Government Resources

Many government programs offer support to businesses like yours. Explore available resources and tap into their expertise to accelerate your growth.

Bonus Step: Continuously Learn and Adapt

The business world is constantly evolving. Stay informed about industry trends, acquire new skills, and adapt your strategies to remain competitive.

Thought-Provoking Questions:

1. Are we using the right financial tools and systems to track and manage our money effectively?
2. Do we have a clear and realistic understanding of our burn rate, runway, and future financial needs?
3. Are we allocating our resources efficiently and strategically to maximize our impact and growth?
4. Have we explored all possible funding options (e.g., grants, loans, crowdfunding, angel investors) to support our growth?
5. What are our biggest financial risks, and what steps can we take to mitigate them?
6. Are we effectively managing our cash flow and ensuring we have enough working capital to meet our obligations?

7. Are we investing enough in research and development to stay ahead of the competition?
8. Are we spending money on the right things, or are there areas where we can cut costs without compromising our goals?
9. How can we better incentivize employees to be cost-conscious and maximize the value they contribute?
10. What are the key financial metrics we should be tracking regularly to measure our progress and identify areas for improvement?

Taking control of your finances and building a strong foundation for global market success is within your grasp by following these steps.

Financial management is a continuous journey, so commit to ongoing learning, adaptation, and making informed decisions.

"How many millionaires do you know who have become wealthy by investing in savings accounts? I rest my case."

— Robert G. Allen

Tools & Resources for Aspiring Entrepreneurs

This section provides a comprehensive list of resources, services, and programs designed to facilitate your entrepreneurial journey.

Focusing primarily on free tools and equipment, we've also included valuable paid options for your consideration.

As you explore this list, you'll discover a mix of free and paid resources, allowing you to choose the most suitable support for your business needs.

1 – Idea Development Tools

Tools and equipment with which you can record and develop your product ideas.

NAME	WHAT IS IT USED FOR?	ADDRESS
milanote	It is a nice application where you can visually organize, store and organize your ideas and projects.	milanote.com
Creatlr	You can open visual thinking records with the people you work with.	creatlr.com
noisli	It helps create the environment they are accustomed to for people who can be creative in noisy and crowded environments.	noisli.com
coggle	You can create brain maps with your colleagues and look for solutions to complex problems.	coggle.it
Idea Lottery	It is a method that allows you to break down the subject you are working on and establish connections between them so that you can find new and creative ideas.	ideachampions.com/ idea_lottery_new.shtml
MindMeister	A brainstorming tool that you can use to create brain maps and visualize your idea.	mindmeister.com
Stormboard	A brainstorming tool where you can collect and vote on your ideas that arise in meetings.	stormboard.com
candor	A free brainstorming management program.	usecandor.com

Creating Minds	It lists methods that will help you think creatively and exemplifies them in detail.	creatingminds.org/tools/tools_ideation.htm
Fast Idea Gen.	It is a method of solving the problem by asking questions that allow you to look at the issue from different perspectives.	diytoolkit.org/tools/fast-idea-generator/

2 – User Experience and Design Tools

Tools and equipment you can use when designing the screens and workflows of your product or service.

NAME	WHAT IS IT USED FOR?	ADDRESS
figma	You can create and manage collaborative design projects with your teammates.	figma.com
photopea	Online graphics program with which you can open and edit PSD, XCF, Sketch (Photoshop, Gimp and Sketch) files. Free.	photopea.com
photo	The site that provides all the most used features in Photoshop online for free and without downloading any program.	fotor.com
Canvas	An online and free graphic editor where you can create wonderful social media visuals without the need for a designer.	canva.com
99Designs	You can meet your logo, corporate identity and similar design needs. You write the brief and choose your favorite among dozens of designers' creations.	99designs.com
FlowMap	You can plan the user experience with the team and extract user flows in detail.	flowmapp.com
whimsical	You can quickly draw user flows, wireframes, post-its and brain maps.	whimsical.com
Marvel	Tool to produce wireframes and prototyping by revising with the team.	marvelapp.com

InVision	A site where you can easily convert the interfaces you design into clickable / navigable prototypes.	invisionapp.com
framer motion	Animation and gesture library that you can create ready for React Native.	framer.com/motion
Lottie	You can easily add animations to mobile applications. If you're animating in After Effects, this is perfect for you.	airbnb.design/lottie
Bot Society	A site where you can easily design and prototype chatbots. Free.	botsociety.io

3 – Software Development Tools

Tools and equipment you can use when designing the screens and workflows of your product or service.

NAME	WHAT IS IT USED FOR?	ADDRESS
thunkable	You can write iOS and Android mobile applications using drag-and-drop without knowing coding.	thunkable.com
bubble	You can develop web programs without needing any technical knowledge.	bubble.io
TellForm	It allows you to create aesthetic forms without the need for coding knowledge. It is an alternative to paid TypeForm.	tellform.com
GraphJS	It allows you to add forum, profile, group, messaging, voting and comment features to your product without coding.	graphjs.com
AMP Validator	It checks that the AMP application you made to open your pages faster in search results is working correctly.	cutt.ly/QyMHxOB
Website Downloader	A site that allows you to download any site you want in its entirety, including articles, images and accessible source codes.	websitedownloader.io
Lazy Load XT	Wordpress plugin that makes your website open faster. It opens your site without waiting for large files such as images, videos, etc. to download.	wordpress.org/plugins/lazy-load-xt
Intro.js	Ready javascript that allows you to show step by step on the interface how your product can be used.	introjs.com

DivJoy	It produces you a ready-made coding foundation for React. It allows you to complete the frontend quickly.	divjoy.com
Find	CSS framework that simplifies frontend software development. Free, open source.	bulding.io

4 – Project Management Tools

The tools and equipment you need to manage daily operations regarding your product.

NAME	WHAT IS IT USED FOR?	ADDRESS
Trello	A free project management tool based on the kanban model that allows you to easily track work.	trello.com
slack	Whatsapp developed for business, which helps you communicate faster with your teammates. Free.	slack.com
Meet	You can easily hold video conferences, meetings and presentations with your colleagues who are far away or in another location. Free.	meet.google.com
Docs	Free Word. You can create, share and edit documents without downloading a program.	google.com/docs
sheets	You can do everything you do in Excel and more. You don't need to install any programs. Free.	google.com/sheets
forms	You can create surveys or forms for free, add them to your site and collect data from people.	google.com/forms
Slides	Free Powerpoint. You can prepare presentations that look very stylish. You can access it from any computer you want.	google.com/slides
Keep	Note-taking product with app and Chrome extension. You can access your notes from any device you want.	google.com/keep

tasks	You can keep your to-do items linked to the calendar and access them from anywhere.	calendar.google.com/calendar/r?opentasks=1&pli=1
conversion	Free online file converter. You can use it to convert a file you have to a different format.	convertio.co
drawing	Graphics creation product where you can create workflows and drawings for free. It works synchronously with Google Drive.	http://draw.io
bionality	Bionluk is a special freelancer platform for startups and businesses.	bionluk.com
Fiverr	You can have all your work done by talented and cheap people on the other side of the world.	fiverr.com
Sticky Notes	A free Google Chrome extension with which you can take Post-it notes.	cutt.ly/hyMH6OF
Streak	CRM solution for Gmail. It organizes all the information about your customers for you without having to search through emails.	streak.com
maildrop	You will be given a free temporary email address and you can check the emails coming to that address without a password. Then that email address is deleted.	maildrop.cc
awesome	You can record screenshots or video while testing the product. You can leave markings and notes on images.	cutt.ly/LyMJiig
Loom	It allows you to record the image of your computer screen as a video and share it easily.	loom.com

Mobile Friendly Test	The site that tells you whether your site is mobile compatible or not and what you need to do to make it better.	search.google.com/test/mobile-friendly
Browser Shots	Site that tests your site in various browsers and resolutions and reports any problems.	browsershots.org
Grammarly	Chrome extension that finds and corrects spelling mistakes in the content you write.	grammarly.com
clockify	It measures how much time you spend on which task through Chrome. It allows you to work more efficiently.	cutt.ly/uyMJdId
StayFocusd	For those who find themselves browsing YouTube and Twitter while trying to get work done, limits discipline.	cutt.ly/byMJgzX
Win the Day	Chrome extension that divides your big goals into daily pieces with a specific completion date and focuses you on the goal.	wintheday.com
Productivity Tracker	If the number of characters you type and the number of links you click are indicators of productivity for you, it will automatically measure your productivity.	cutt.ly/XyMJj78
Calm	A Chrome extension that makes you breathe, refreshes and relaxes you during stressful times.	cutt.ly/5yMJkEt

5 – Marketing Tools

Tools and equipment that will be useful when marketing your product or service and will make your life easier.

NAME	WHAT IS IT USED FOR?	ADDRESS
ubersuggest	A tool where you can get keyword suggestions related to your product.	neilpatel.com/ubersuggest
tawk.to	It allows you to add live chat to your website or mobile application and send marketing messages. Free.	tawk.to
OneSignal	It allows you to send push notifications from your mobile application and website for free.	onesignal.com
namelix	It helps you find global names for your product or company.	namelix.com
Business Name Generator	It makes thousands of suggestions for your company or product in response to a word you give.	businessnamegenerator.com
namemesh	When searching for a domain name, it offers suggestions that are close to yours or better.	namemesh.com
Bust-a-Name	It makes finding domain names easier by performing automatic searches with different combinations.	bustaname.com
Instant Domain Search	A site that allows you to search and find domains very quickly.	instantdomainsearch.com

AppMetrica	It shows the channels from which your application was downloaded and the performance of these channels. Free version of Adjust or Appsflyer.	appmetrica.yandex.com
firebase	A free product with which you can collect all kinds of analytical statistics about your application, A/B test or create marketing messages for the application.	firebase.google.com
AppAnnie	Analysis site that shows Apple and Android applications in which key terms and in which rankings.	appannie.com
Sensor Tower	Analysis site that shows which mobile application is downloaded how many times a month and how much money it makes.	sensortower.com
The Name App	It is useful for finding a name for your product, and also checks whether the domain of the name you found is empty.	thenameapp.com
revue	It allows you to prepare free newsletters and send them to your followers' e-mail addresses.	getrevue.co
submit.co	The site that shows all the addresses and emails where you can get news or review of your product.	submit.co
PRLog	A site that saves and distributes your press release to hundreds of news sources for free.	prlog.org
Yoast SEO	Wordpress plugin that measures how successful the article you write for your website is in terms of SEO and offers suggestions.	wordpress.org/plugins/wordpress-seo

Anchor	It allows you to make a podcast with professional sound effects about your product and publish it for free on iTunes, Spotify, etc.	anchor.fm
Make My Persona	You can create detailed customer profiles for segmentation.	hubspot.com/make-my-persona

Global Entrepreneur's Library

I n this section, you will find the books and resources you must read to become a global entrepreneur.

Taken as reference, which were useful in the creation of this book .

NAME OF THE BOOK	SUBJECT	AUTHOR
A Dream of Turkey	It examines down - to - earth ideas for the total development of Turkey.	Selçuk R. Şirin
Here are the Gazelles	The stories of dozens of different paths to success from Turkey's most important entrepreneurs.	Erhan Erkut, Dilek Özmen
The Four Steps to the Epiphany	Strategies for successful startups. The book is the creator of the "Lean Startup" concept.	Steve Blank
hooked	Ways to create addictive digital products.	Nir Eyal

Made to Stick	Why do some business ideas and companies survive for many years, but others die?	Chip Heath
The Automatic Customer	developing a subscription-based business model for any industry.	John Warrillow
Creative Confidence	It tells us that we can all actually develop creative ideas.	Tom Kelley
The Startup Owner's Manual	Ways to create a successful enterprise step by step.	Steve Blank
The Lean Entrepreneur	How visionary entrepreneurs develop products and become market leaders.	Brant Cooper
Global Product Development	Things that need to be taken into consideration in order to develop quality products that can be offered to the whole world.	Alain Bernard
Global Marketing	International marketing strategies and sales development methods.	Warren Keegan, Mark Green
Global Product	A guide to creating products that are successful in multiple countries.	John Stark
Global Brand Power	Ways to create a globally recognized brand.	Barbara E. Kahn
Flow	It tells us that achieving success at work and happiness in life requires being in "flow".	Mihaly Csikszentmihalyi
Nudge	It explains that people's daily decisions can be changed with very small touches.	Richard H. Thaler
Creating Breakthrough Products	on the secret tactics that trigger global innovation.	J. Cagan, C. M. Vogel
The Hard Thing About Hard Things	How Ben Horowitz, one of Silicon Valley's most important names, invests, manages and sells.	Ben Horowitz

Title	Description	Author
Strategic New Product Development for the Global Economy	New product development methods compatible with international economic balances.	Toyohiro Kono, Leonard Lynn
The Design Thinking Playbook	Adaptation of teams, products, services and business models to digital transformation.	Michael Lewrick
Design Sprint	It focuses on a way of doing business that has become very popular in the software world.	Richard Banfield
Project to Product	What it takes to design products that can continue to succeed in the digital world.	Mik Kersten
Escaping the Build Trap	How to do effective product management that actually provides a benefit?	Melissa Perri
The Lean Startup	The way of doing business : How do today's entrepreneurs create extremely successful products?	Eric Ries
The Inevitable	To better understand the technological forces shaping our future.	kevin kelly
Predictably Irrational	It tells us how strange the decisions people make in their daily lives are.	Dan Ariely
The Purpose Economy	It shows how people united around a cause can create great economic values.	Aaron Hurst
The Startup Playbook	Secret tactics of the founders of fast-growing startups.	David Kidder
The Obstacle Is the Way	It tells how people who have dealt with difficulties for a long time can achieve great victories.	Ryan Holiday
The 4-Hour Workweek	Establishing companies that operate on their own without you and have no salaried employees.	Timothy Ferriss

Field Guide to Human-Centered Design	Product development methods and user experience processes that focus on people.	IDEO
Reality Is Broken	It explains how people can change the world through gamification.	Jane McGonigal
Gamification by Design	It focuses on how gamification can be integrated into business models.	Gabe Zichermann
The Upside of Irrationality	It explains how non-rational human decisions can actually lead to better results.	Dan Ariely
Fun Inc.	He emphasizes that the game will dominate the 21st century and change our lifestyles.	Tom Chatfield
Manage Your Day-to-Day	focuses on the routines and focus methods you need to create to increase your work efficiency.	Jocelyn K. Glei
rework	It describes the intricacies of working remotely and how to achieve success faster.	Jason Fried
Tools of Titans	Tactics, routines and habits of successful business people.	Timothy Ferriss
Business Model You	It allows you to design yourself like a business model and plan your future better.	Tim Clark
The Medici Effect	epidemics and elephants teach us about innovation?	Frans Johansson
Transform Your Habits	Creating habits that lead to success and ensuring they are permanent.	James Clear
Expert Secrets	It tells how experts in the business world create successful careers for themselves.	Russell Brunson
Thinking, Fast and Slow	It teaches us to use the fast and slow-thinking parts of our brain more efficiently.	Daniel Kahneman

Start with Why	It tells us that there is always a greater purpose behind successful work.	Simon Sinek
The Tipping Point	It explains how small details lead to big results.	Malcolm Gladwell
Creative Selection	Details of Apple's design processes during the time of Steve Job .	Ken Kocienda
Creativity Inc.	Ways to remove the obstacles to your creativity, one by one.	Ed Catmull, Amy Wallace
Steal Like an Artist	He argues that at the core of all great innovations are traces of old great ideas.	Austin Kleon
Curious	He talks about the effect of being curious in making a person successful.	Ian Leslie
thinkpak	A book consisting of brainstorming cards developed to find creative ideas.	Michael Michalko
The Creativity Challenge	It consists of exercises that will increase our creativity and keep our brain fresh.	Tanner Christensen
365	Every day of the year , we take on and carry out a task that will trigger our creativity.	Noah Scalin
Orbiting The Giant Hairball	It offers creativity exercises in different forms.	Gordon Mackenzie
thinkertoys	It deals with creative thinking methods in detail.	Michael Michalko
Mastering Creativity	It focuses on the path to being creative and its various methods.	James Clear
Team Genius	focuses on the team required to be successful, the characteristics of this team and how it can be established.	Rich Karlgaard

creativity	It focuses on the psychological details behind great inventions and inventions.	Mihaly Csikszentmihalyi
This is Marketing	Lists what the new rules of marketing are in the changing digital world.	Seth Godin
Getting Started with Growth Hacking	talks about ways to grow an enterprise without spending too much money.	Muhammed Tüfekyapan
Lean Analytics	How can we establish more successful ventures using business data?	Alistair Croll, Ben Yoskovitz
23 Visual Principles	Things to consider when designing "opening" pages where the customer encounters our product for the first time.	Oli Gardner
Tribes	What needs to be done to promote an extraordinary idea and increase the number of people who believe in this idea.	Seth Godin
100 Days of Growth	It focuses on fast, economical and effective marketing methods.	Sujan Patel
Designing for Behavior Change	Ways to design products that are powerful enough to cause behavioral change.	Stephen Wendel
Landing Page Secrets	Features of landing pages that provide very good conversions.	Rajat Arora
Traction	All marketing methods and details that can be used to gain new customers for a startup.	Gabriel Weinberg
Startup Growth Engines	Successful ventures and the marketing tactics that helped them grow.	Sean Ellis
The Myths of Innovation	It focuses on common misconceptions about innovation.	Scott Berkun
The Ten Faces of Innovation	What it takes to build innovative businesses.	Tom Kelley

Title	Description	Author
Inside Real Innovation	How crazy ideas in the research and development process turn into business models that find a place in the market.	Eugene Fitzgerald
The Innovator's Dilemma	What companies pursuing innovation may lose while pursuing new ideas.	M. Clayton Christensen
Innovation Teams	Ways and must - haves to build a team that makes innovation possible.	Nesta
App Secrets	Tactics that make mobile applications popular and successful.	Sean Casto
Delivering Happiness	Ways to find income, passion and purpose, from the founder of the shoe company Zappos.	Tony Hsieh
Built to Last	Habits of large companies that have survived successfully for many years.	Jim Collins, Jerry I. Porras
Zero to One	Explanation with examples on turning a business idea into a successful venture.	Peter Thiel
Entrepreneurs Guide to Customer Development	He argues that a company can only be successful if it understands its customers perfectly. It focuses on the concept of "customer discovery".	Brant Cooper & Patrick Vlaskovits
Making Digital Work	A systematic process on how digital products should be implemented.	Nesta
Business Model Generation	Tactics for finding the most suitable commercial model of a product and increasing sales.	Alexander Osterwalder
Prototyping Framework	Ways to design an idea in the smallest form that can be presented to the customer.	Nesta
Making Ideas Happen	Ways to achieve success by establishing a strong connection between vision and realities.	Scott Belsky

Title	Description	Author
Inspired	How to develop technology products that customers will fall in love with?	Marty Cagan
The Future of Design	Innovation for the product that can achieve global success in our complex world.	LorraineJustice
Magnetic Marketing	Ways to find loyal and recommending customers who do not hesitate to give money.	Dan S. Kennedy
Building Digital Products	Digital product development methods and tactics.	Alex Mitchell
Think Like a Freak	A fascinating book that shows what great economic opportunities exist at the intersection of sociology and marketing.	Steven D. Levitt
Don't Make Me Think	It explains that a good user experience is a design that requires minimum effort from the customer.	Steve Krug
100 Things Every Designer Needs to Know about People	focuses on the fact that making a good design requires understanding people well.	Susan M. Weinschenk
The Halo Effect	It focuses on our "manager" ego, which stands as a major obstacle to increasing the performance of the business we manage.	Philip M. Rosenzweig

PLEASE, LEAVE A REVIEW

Did this book help you in some way? If so, I'd love to hear about it.

Honest reviews help readers find the right book for their needs.

Good reviews connect readers to great books, and your voice matters.

To leave a review, please search the name of the book on amazon.com.

Thanks for being part of the journey!

Printed in Great Britain
by Amazon